Courtesy National Park Service, Statue of Liberty National Monument

THE
STATUE OF LIBERTY REVISITED

EDITED BY WILTON S. DILLON
& NEIL G. KOTLER

SMITHSONIAN INSTITUTION PRESS • WASHINGTON AND LONDON

Copy Editor: Jan McInroy
Production Editor: Jenelle Walthour
Designer: Linda McKnight

Library of Congress Cataloging-in-Publication Data
The Statue of Liberty revisited : making a universal symbol /
    edited by Wilton S. Dillon and Neil G. Kotler.
        p.   cm.
    Includes bibliographical references.
    ISBN 1-56098-252-7 (alk. paper)
        1. Statue of Liberty (New York, N.Y.) 2. New York
    (N.Y.)—Buildings, structures, etc. 3. United States—
    Emigration and Immigration. 4. Women—United
    States—Social conditions.   I. Dillon, Wilton.
    II. Kotler, Neil G., 1941–
    F128.64.L6S73   1993
    974.7'1—dc20   92-37913

British Library Cataloguing-in-Publication Data is available

Manufactured in the United States of America
∞ 99 98 97 96 95 94 5 4 3 2 1

⊗ The paper used in this publication meets the minimum re-
quirements of the American National Standard for Permanence
of Paper for Printed Library Materials Z39.48-1984.

Jacket photo by Alan Shortall, courtesy of Chermayeff and
Geismar, Inc.

*To Virginia and Harris Dillon
and
Wendy and Jena Kotler*

CONTENTS

Acknowledgments

The starting point for this volume of essays was the initiative of Edouard-René Lefebvre de Laboulaye, who first conceived the idea of a gift to the United States that eventually took the form of the Statue of Liberty. His illustrious descendants, the father and son diplomats Andrew de Laboulaye and François de Laboulaye, have kept her flame burning ever since.

Anticipating the centennial of the Statue of Liberty in 1986, Wilton S. Dillon of the Smithsonian Institution organized and chaired a symposium with the title "Liberty: As Idea, Icon, and Engineering Feat," held at the Cooper-Hewitt Museum in New York on October 19, 1985.

The core of this volume is the essays that were presented at that event, which have since been updated and further enriched by new materials. Missing here, however, are the rich insights of some of the symposiasts: Ross Holland, a former United States Park Service official who spoke on the sense of place, the site, and the restoration; Harold Pfister, of the Cooper-Hewitt Museum, who extended hospitable greetings to the assembly; Mary Ann Harrell and Alan Kraut, who authored the National Geographic Society book *Liberty: The Statue and the American Dream;* the late Cynthia Jaffe

McCabe, of the Hirshhorn Museum and Sculpture Garden, who illustrated how the statue has become an icon in modern art; Edward L. Kallop, Jr., of the National Park Service, who showed slides of replicas and models of the statue that exist in different parts of the United States and the world; Eric DeLony, who delivered a comprehensive account of the use of photography to document the National Park Service's historic restoration of the statue; and Kenneth L. Burns, who commented on and screened for the group his documentary film *The Statue of Liberty*, which has since become a part of his prizewinning legacy of films shown in retrospectives after his 1990 *Civil War* made him a household name.

The late Dorothy Richardson of the Smithsonian made arrangements for the participants to dine at the top of the World Trade Center, in a restaurant called Windows on the World, looking down upon the statue in New York Harbor. Afterwards, the symposiasts boarded the Staten Island ferry for a nocturnal view of the statue, which at that time was under renovation and surrounded by scaffolding. The New York Historical Society and the French Cultural Counsellor feted the guests at receptions on opposite sides of Central Park.

In Paris, the Smithsonian's representative, Sir Valentine Abdy, interceded with French museums and libraries in search of illustrations. The founder of Les Amis Français de la Smithsonian, Francois E. Pinson, provided invaluable liaison services. Dominique Sur arranged for an inspection of the site in Paris where the statue was built. Eugenie Angles made available resources at the Musée Blérancourt. French Cultural Services in New York also made helpful intercessions.

Special thanks go to Barry Moreno and Jeff Dosik, librarians at the Statue of Liberty National Monument, and to their colleagues Sydney Onikul and Felice Ciccione, curators at the monument. Archivists at the New York Historical Society, the Museum of the City of New York, and the New York Public Library also provided assistance.

At the Smithsonian, Carla M. Borden, of the Office of Interdisciplinary Studies, provided vital expertise in publishing and also contributed materials on Emma Lazarus. For ideas on both substance and style, Mark G. Hirsch, acquisitions editor for American studies at the Smithsonian Institution Press, deserves praise. Mary Lynne McElroy and Taneesha V. Barnes patiently labored to prepare the manuscript. Astrophysicist Frederic H. Chaffee, a member of the Smithsonian's Whipple Observatory, conducted an initial recorded interview with Professor Fang Li Zhi, his colleague at the University of Arizona. Smithsonian volunteer Mildred Hall provided an excellent transcript of that interview. Thomas Lawton, of the Sackler and the Freer galleries at the Smithsonian, helped us to make contact with Tsao Hsingyuan and arrange for the publication of her extraordinary account of the construction in Beijing, China, of the Goddess of Democracy, and Professor James Cahill, in the Department of the History of Art at the University of California, Berkeley, was extremely helpful in preparing the essay for publication. James H. Wallace, Jr., and his colleagues at the Smithsonian's photographic services office documented Liberty's 1986 centennial celebration. The Smithson Society provided generous support for the 1985 symposium and for the preparation of this volume.

The editors are grateful to all others who continue to provide answers to the questions raised at the 1985 centennial symposium: What does the statue mean for intellectual history, popular culture, civics, and diplomacy, among other topics? What is the role of symbols in thought and life? How does Liberty shed light on gift behavior among peoples and nations? How does an abstract idea such as "liberty" translate into and manifest itself in different cultures? What plans should be made now to celebrate Liberty's bicentennial in the year 2086?

The Statue of Liberty as Idea, Symbol, and Historical Presence

NEIL G. KOTLER

y American," she was called by her creator, the French sculptor Frédéric-Auguste Bartholdi.

With her torch rising 305 feet above New York Harbor, the Statue of Liberty was, at the official unveiling on October 28, 1886, the tallest structure in the Americas—taller even than the just-completed Brooklyn Bridge standing at the harbor's entrance. One hundred years later, the statue no longer could claim distinction for its physical size, yet its grandeur as a symbol had transformed it into one of the most venerated monuments in all of world history.

The statue's very existence, however, was never assured. Had it not been for the determination of a handful of committed individuals, the outpouring of public support in France and in the United States, and a combination of lucky circumstances, the statue might never have seen the light of day. Human error, even natural disasters, nearly prevented its realization.

Twenty-one years elapsed between the genesis of the idea for the statue and its completion in New York Harbor; eleven of those years involved the work of design and construction. The entire project depended on the donations of ordinary French citizens, who contributed more than 400,000 francs.

Even as the statue was being loaded onto a ship in France for its journey to the United States, the fundraising campaign to build the pedestal stalled. For nearly a year the pieces of the statue sat in the 210 wooden crates in which they had been transported to Bedloe's Island, because money for constructing the base of the monument had run out. The greatest test during the twenty-one years probably occurred at sea: the ship carrying the statue across the Atlantic Ocean nearly capsized during a storm.

Yet the Statue of Liberty prevailed against the odds and the elements, and the day of its official opening arrived. New Yorkers lined the gaily festooned waterfront on the rainy, overcast day, gazing across the harbor at the dimly lit contours of Liberty. New York City declared the day a public holiday, and tens of thousands of New Yorkers paraded down Broadway.

United States president Grover Cleveland officiated at the opening ceremonies at Bedloe's Island. A veritable armada of ships sailed into New York Harbor on that day, among them a small boat chartered by women known as suffragists. Their boat circled the statue many times while the women aboard used a megaphone to hurl harsh words at the officials and guests who had gathered for the ceremony. Demanding equal treatment for women, the suffragists seized on the fact that only two of the nearly six hundred people invited to witness the ceremonial unveiling of Liberty were women, even though the symbol that they had gathered to honor was profoundly female in character (fig. 1.1).

A high point in the ceremony was the president's remarks. Bartholdi, the statue's creator, looked down upon the crowd from inside the statue, which he called Liberty Enlightening the World, and President Cleveland said to the assembled guests: "We will not forget that Liberty has made here her home.... Reflected thence and joined with answering rays, a stream of light shall pierce the darkness of ignorance and man's oppression until Liberty enlightens the world."

"Imposing ... she looked imposing," recalled a professor in Boston who, after a difficult ocean voyage as a child in the 1950s, walked onto the deck of the ship in early morning and stared in awe at the 225-ton statue.

"From childhood when I was in Tabriz, Iran," Vartan Gregori-

Fig. 1.1. The Inauguration of the Statue of Liberty, known as Liberty Enlightening the World, October 28, 1886. This photograph, by H. O'Neil, was taken from the steamer *Patrol* in New York Harbor. The arrival of President Grover Cleveland at Bedloe's Island (later renamed Liberty Island) was accompanied by a naval salute from the ships offshore. Reprinted by permission of Library of Congress, Washington, D.C.

an, president of Brown University, told Ken Burns, producer of a celebrated film on the Statue of Liberty, "on the U.S. stamps and everything was the Statue of Liberty and I had a very idealized notion of America. . . . [E]ven though years later I went to school and learned about nuances, ambiguities, shades and all kinds of shadows the Statue of Liberty had, the first day that I approached New York it was a shattering experience for me to find that a whole nation was welcoming me spiritually to a new land."

Edith Hartmann, an immigrant from Europe, also recalled her first view of Liberty. "I went through hell in Europe," she recounted. "My grandparents and my only brother were taken to a concentration camp. . . . [We were] lucky enough and fortunate enough to get a visa to this country. . . . And when I first saw the Statue of Lib-

3

erty, I broke down in tears and I could have fallen on my knees and kissed the ground. . . . I was fortunate enough to reach this blessed country."

This collection of essays first took shape in a Smithsonian Institution colloquium held in New York City to commemorate the one hundredth anniversary of Liberty's unveiling. Events and expectations during the first hundred years of the statue's existence have continually recast its meaning and symbolism. These essays take a fresh, new look at Liberty—exploring not only its origins, development, and historical significance but also its iconography, politics, and the remarkable influence that the Statue of Liberty exerts on other peoples of the world.

In preparing the book, the editors glimpsed yet another emanation of Liberty's symbolic force—this time from halfway around the world. In a five-day period in the summer of 1989, a large statue known as the Goddess of Democracy was erected in the center of Beijing, the capital city of the People's Republic of China. Its resemblance and the influence it owed to the Statue of Liberty were unmistakable.

LIBERTY REBORN IN CHINA AS THE GODDESS OF DEMOCRACY

For five days, between May 30 and June 4, 1989, visitors to Tiananmen Square in the center of Beijing witnessed an unusual sight. Standing close to one of the gates that opened onto the square was a statue of Styrofoam plastic and plaster, approximately ten meters tall, a chalk-white female figure draped in a robe, with her two arms thrust above her head and holding a torch (fig. 1.2).

Surrounded by young people who formed an honor guard, the Goddess stood opposite a huge color portrait depicting Mao Tse-tung, the founder of Communist China, who died in 1976. Never before could the residents of Beijing recall seeing such a spectacle: a statue symbolizing the yearning for freedom and democracy placed alongside the image of China's revolutionary dictator, a figure that inspired the utmost fear.

The Beijing statue was created by students who had organized a pro-democracy demonstration against the Chinese government,

Fig. 1.2. Goddess of Democracy. During the student pro-democracy demonstrations in 1989 in Tiananmen Square in Beijing, capital of the People's Republic of China, a protester holds up two flags on a platform next to the statue that became the Goddess of Democracy, the most prominent symbol of the demonstrations. This photograph, by Fumiyo Asahi, was taken on Wednesday morning, May 31. Reprinted by permission of Reuters/Bettmann.

demanding political reforms and personal liberties. The statue symbolized the yearning for freedom among ordinary Chinese people; its resemblance to the Statue of Liberty was intentional, not accidental.

LIBERTY AT THE CREATION

From its very beginnings, the Statue of Liberty was designed to be a beacon, a universal symbol, for the spread of freedom and self-government everywhere. Bartholdi was convinced that if the statue were built in the United States, in the New World, it would serve to arouse the love for liberty and free government in the Old World. Upon the statue's completion in the spring of 1884, Bartholdi observed: "I will try to glorify the republic and liberty over there [in

America] in the hope that someday I will find it again here in France."

The Statue of Liberty, the world's most celebrated symbol of American freedom and democracy, was first conceived overseas in the summer of 1865, by a group of Frenchmen at a dinner party near Versailles, outside of Paris. France at the time was ruled by the dictator Napoleon III. The individuals gathered that evening were political reformers, liberals, and democrats who were vocal opponents of Napoleon's harsh and repressive government. The host of the dinner party was Edouard-René Lefebvre de Laboulaye, professor of law at the Collège de France, author of several books on American law and history, and a prominent liberal leader who admired the United States as a model of liberty and self-government.

Laboulaye had attracted a considerable following among students and intellectuals in championing the example of the United States and the cause of French-American cooperation. The Union victory over the Confederacy that year and the abolition of slavery reinforced the view in France that the United States would become an important ally in the struggle for freedom throughout the world. The assassination of President Abraham Lincoln in 1865, therefore, was an event that caused great anguish.

As an expression of French sympathies for the slain American president, Laboulaye's circle agreed to send Mrs. Lincoln a gift of a gold medal, with the inscription "Lincoln, an honest man; abolished slavery, saved the republic, and was assassinated on the 15th of April, 1865." Laboulaye then proposed to his guests that a more substantial gift to the American people be found to coincide with the centennial celebration of American independence that would take place ten years later. Laboulaye thought a gift would bolster the relationship between the two countries and solidify American support for the French struggle to restore self-government.

Bartholdi, a young, ambitious French sculptor, was present at the dinner party, having just been commissioned to create a bust of the host, Laboulaye. As an artist devoted to building huge public monuments, Bartholdi volunteered himself to create a statue that would realize Laboulaye's gift. That evening's discussion paved the way for the decision to build a statue honoring America that would be situated in New York.

LIBERTY AS A SYMBOL OF FRENCH AND AMERICAN FRIENDSHIP

The Statue of Liberty originated as a gift to symbolize the friendship of France and the United States. Indeed, the close relationship and even interdependence between the two peoples dated back to the earliest settlement in North America. One hundred years before American independence, Frenchmen were among the first Europeans to explore and settle the North American continent. Louis Jolliet and Jacques Marquette traveled the Mississippi River in the 1670s. René Robert Cavelier, Sieur de La Salle, explored the Great Lakes and then established a colony in what became Louisiana. Pierre Le Moyne, Sieur d'Iberville, built a French outpost on the Gulf of Mexico, at Biloxi, Mississippi, and his brother, Jean Baptiste Le Moyne, Sieur de Bienville, founded New Orleans. Between the 1680s and 1748, France colonized a great land mass stretching north into eastern Canada, in what was called New France, and reaching south into the territory of Louisiana.

The prominent French leader Marquis de Lafayette fought at the side of General George Washington in the American War of Independence. Thomas Jefferson, a lifelong admirer of French science and technology, succeeded Benjamin Franklin as the American minister to France. At the close of the War of Independence, a French military force led by General Jean Baptiste de Rochambeau, as well as a French naval force, fought alongside Americans in the final campaign against the British, which culminated in the British defeat at the Battle of Yorktown in 1781. Historians have asserted that without French assistance and support, the American Republic might not have gained its independence.

In the twentieth century, it should be noted, the United States provided invaluable support to the French people. In the two world wars, American soldiers fought alongside the French, and in World War II, American and British military forces liberated France from Nazi German occupation.

The French political reformers who conceived of a gift to the American people, a gift that eventually became the Statue of Liberty, were seeking a powerful symbol that would reinvigorate a long-standing friendship and partnership. Indeed, Liberty ultimately succeeded in demonstrating the historic interdependence between the two peoples. The statue itself was created by a French sculptor and built by a French engineer and work force. The pedestal on which the statue rests was designed by an American architect, Richard Morris Hunt, who took his training at the famous art school, l'école nationale supérieure des Beaux-Arts, in Paris. The money to pay for the statue was raised by French citizens and French businesses. But it was an American immigrant, Joseph Pulitzer, publisher of the *New York World* and the *St. Louis Post-Dispatch* newspapers, who spearheaded the American fundraising campaign to finance Liberty's pedestal. Meeting widespread skepticism and even indifference at first, Pulitzer's efforts finally yielded $250,000 in donations for the pedestal, making the monument's completion possible.

LIBERTY'S IMAGE AND SYMBOLISM

The Statue of Liberty is an amalgam of ideas and images that took shape principally in the artistic imagination of Frédéric-Auguste Bartholdi. Laboulaye worked closely with Bartholdi on the form of the future monument. In 1849 Laboulaye had begun a three-volume *History of the United States*, which was published in France in 1866, one year after the gift idea was introduced. For Laboulaye and other liberal intellectuals, the founding of the United States represented a watershed event for the spread of freedom and self-government in the modern world. In his writings he referred to the American nation as "the dawn of a new world. . . . [I]t was liberty that rose on the other side of the Atlantic to enlighten . . . the universe." In Laboulaye's mind the future monument in America should convey the idea that the United States was the world's beacon and prime guardian of liberty. The American people, he understood, were ever ready to come to the aid of other nations in their struggle to establish freedom and democratic government. One other idea of Laboulaye's was critical to the design of a monument to freedom: to safeguard freedom, government has to operate according to laws and constitutional authority.

Bartholdi was a great admirer of the classical art of ancient Greece and ancient Rome, and classical imagery played an important part in his sculpture. In the ancient world, before the Christian era, female figures had been used in art, literature, and mythology to represent the ideals of truth, faith, wisdom, and liberty. One of the earliest pieces of art, known as the Goddess of Liberty, depicted a robed figure crowned with a bonnet, holding a scepter at her side, with a cat at her feet. This famous statue stood in Rome in the third century B.C. It symbolized emancipation from slavery (a common institution in ancient times), the personal freedoms that an individual can enjoy, and belief in the divine protection of individuals who made the passage from slavery to freedom.

Another key element in Bartholdi's art was his admiration for large-scale monuments that stood in unobstructed public spaces and that could inspire a sense of awe in masses of people. Public art was widely celebrated in nineteenth-century Europe, and its creators and sponsors held the view that such art can serve as a device for awakening popular support for and identification with political leaders, movements, parties, and ideals.

Finally, a third key element influenced Bartholdi's design. The idea that a statue could symbolize enlightenment, human and social progress, was embedded in modern French history. The eighteenth century in France was known as the Age of Enlightenment. This era celebrated the flowering of science and technology, the belief in progress, and the ability to reform society and expand individual freedom. A dominant idea held that all human beings derived from a common origin and were involved in a shared destiny. It was widely believed that civilization, like rays of the sun, would spread from one nation to another and ultimately become a universal ideal honored throughout the world.

Bartholdi was already working on a monument in Egypt at the time he was planning a design for a monument in the United States. The Suez Canal, connecting the Mediterranean Sea at one end with the Red Sea and the Indian Ocean at the other, was opened in 1869. Two years earlier, Bartholdi had proposed to the leader of Egypt a design for a lighthouse that would stand at the canal's entrance; he called it "Progress" or "Egypt Bringing the Light to Asia."

In ancient times, the entryway to a harbor was often adorned with a huge statue of a male or female figure built on top of a lighthouse-type structure, symbolizing both the greatness of the nation and the guardian spirit that illuminated and protected the passage of ships. The largest such statue was situated in the harbor of the Greek island of Rhodes in the third century B.C. The Colossus of Rhodes was a representation of the Greek god Helios, and it served as an inspiration for Bartholdi and later became one of the major in-fluences on the Statue of Liberty.

Bartholdi's Suez Canal project was never undertaken, however. The ruler of Egypt at the time was either unwilling or unable to commit adequate funds to the project, and it got no further than the clay models in the sculptor's workshop. Once Bartholdi abandoned plans for the Egyptian monument, he was free to work on an American monument. His drawings for the Statue of Liberty do bear a resemblance to his drawings for the Suez Canal statue. His great passion for public monuments was readily transferred from the Egyptian project to the American one.

Bartholdi traveled to the United States in 1871, his first visit to the New World. Standing on a small island in New York Harbor known as Bedloe's Island, Bartholdi formed an image of the statue in his mind. Later he wrote to his patron, Laboulaye: "If I myself felt that spirit here, then it is certainly here that my statue must rise; here where people get their first view of the New World, and where liberty casts her rays on both worlds."

The Statue of Liberty in its final form synthesized the ideas and images that Bartholdi and Laboulaye sought to communicate to the peoples of the United States and France. Its protean quality exceed-ed even their ambitious vision. The statue was a gift without parallel between two nations, a monument of breathtaking proportions, a sign of a historical era's struggle for freedom and democracy, and a grand symbol depicting timeless and universal human aspirations.

CONSTRUCTING THE STATUE

The actual construction of the statue was made possible by the great engineering innovations of the last half of the nineteenth century. Technology had become an important measure of human progress. Nations competed with one another in international fairs, display-ing the latest machines, which came to symbolize national power. Railroads in the United States and in Europe were expanding their reach. Internal-combustion engines were the pride of the industrial countries; United States president Ulysses S. Grant proudly showed off the new Corliss engine at Philadelphia's Centennial Exposition in 1876. The Garabit Viaduct in France, a railroad bridge spanning 544 feet with a single arch, was a masterpiece of engineering de-

Fig. 1.3. A stage in the construction of the Statue of Liberty. This 1882 photograph shows the lath foundation of the statue's left hand, which is being cast in plaster. Liberty's creator, Frédéric-Auguste Bartholdi, appears hatless in the right foreground. The original photograph appeared in the 1883 collection of the Frédéric A. Bartholdi Album des Travaux de Construction de la Statue Colossale de la Liberté, Musée Bartholdi, Colmar, France. Reprinted by permission of Library of Congress, Washington, D.C.

signed by Gustave Eiffel. In the United States the Brooklyn Bridge, with its unprecedented span of 1,600 feet connecting the cities of Brooklyn and New York, was designed by John Augustus Roebling and opened with great fanfare in 1883.

Constructing the Statue of Liberty in New York Harbor presented a special set of engineering challenges (fig. 1.3). The exterior skin of copper had to be fastened to an internal support system, and both had to withstand the vertical force of gravity as well as the horizontal force of the high winds that buffeted the harbor. Bartholdi selected France's leading structural engineer, Eugène Emmanuel Viollet-le-Duc, to supervise the statue's construction. When Viollet-le-Duc died unexpectedly in 1879, the work was turned over to French engineer Gustave Eiffel, a celebrated figure who was credited with such major innovations as continuous girder construction of bridges and the use of iron pylons to support his structures. Eiffel's most famous work, the Eiffel Tower in Paris, was opened in 1889, three years after the opening of the Statue of Liberty. Eiffel set out to create an interior structure consisting of a lightweight trusswork, the supports of which were attached by thin, flat bars, springs, and bolts to the statue's copper skin. Eiffel's ingenious engineering provided both resilience and rigid structural support.

PERSPECTIVES ON THE STATUE OF LIBERTY

This volume examines the history of the Statue of Liberty and its significance: why the statue was created; who influenced its development and design; how it was engineered and built; what factors shaped the popular perceptions of Liberty and the changes these perceptions have undergone; what fundamental truths are embodied in the statue; and why the statue has captured the imagination of peoples everywhere.

Seymour Drescher places the Statue of Liberty in the philosophical and political context of French politics and ideology during the latter half of the nineteenth century. Drescher's essay highlights the considerable influence of American liberalism on French politics. Christian Blanchet probes the universal appeal of the Statue of Liberty and its adaptability to events and changes in history. Rudolph J. Vecoli takes as his point of departure Emma Lazarus's celebrated poem honoring the statue, "The New Colossus," and explores Liberty's meaning for generations of European immigrants who first viewed their new homeland from New York Harbor. Bertrand Dard examines the symbolic richness and the iconography of the Statue of Liberty. David P. Billington surveys the engineering and construction of the statue in the context of the great engineering breakthroughs of the nineteenth century.

In addition to the original essays, the editors incorporated two new chapters, exploring a range of contemporary ideas about the Statue of Liberty. Fang Li Zhi, the distinguished Chinese physicist and human rights advocate, probes the meaning of the statue in relation to the struggle for freedom and human rights in China. Tsao Hsingyuan's narrative focuses on the construction of the Goddess of Democracy in Beijing and its linkages to Western ideals. The essay "Everybody's Gal," by Barbara A. Babcock and John J. MacAloon, tells the fascinating story of the use and meaning of female and maternal images throughout history in depicting human ideals, yielding new insights into the symbolism and politics of the Statue of Liberty. The essay reflects upon an irony of iconographic history. Artists, and often the political leaders and institutions sponsoring their work, readily make use of female images in sculpture and painting not as subjects in their own right but as instrumental values, representations of something else—e.g., a human value such as liberty, justice, peace. The irony becomes full-blown when one considers, historically, that women were not often allowed to work as artists or to assume roles of political authority or, for that matter, to write history from a women's point of view. The world of art and the world of power, in other words, for much of history were male worlds, as was the case at the 1886 inauguration of the Statue of Liberty in New York Harbor, when a ceremonial gathering of some six hundred persons led by the president of the United States included only two female participants. Babcock and MacAloon offer a challenging analysis of the role of women as representational images in art and politics as well as the image of the female in the Statue of Liberty itself.

It should be noted, however, that in interpreting the Statue of Liberty as a female image, other points of view regarding the treatment of the female warrant consideration. One such contrasting view is presented by Kathleen Chevalier, who teaches "Gender in Renaissance Art," a course at the American College in Paris. In personal correspondence with the editors, Ms. Chevalier writes:

> When looking for gender-related issues in art, I tend to disregard allegorical figures. . . . [W]hen the concepts embodied related directly to the traditionally male spheres (law, justice, force, etc.), the female figures do not usually bring into play what was projected as their "feminine qualities" (chaste refinement, delicate beauty, provocative eroticism, etc.). . . . I looked at the Statue of Liberty for the first time in ages, and I was struck by her gender-neutral appearance. Is she really a woman? . . . Neither virgin, nor wife, nor mother, nor widow; rather, abstract and frigid. . . . an armed non-woman with whom men certainly would prefer not to mess.

Wilton S. Dillon's concluding essay, "The Ultimate Gift," places the Statue of Liberty in the context of more than two hundred years of "gift exchange" between France and the United States. What originated as a gift between two peoples became transformed into the premier icon of the contemporary world.

THE STATUE OF LIBERTY'S HISTORICAL SIGNIFICANCE

Bartholdi's Statue of Liberty, in its formal design, drew upon the great historical images and ideals in statuary and monumental art that first appeared in ancient times. The statue was envisioned as a relatively traditional form on an imposing physical scale. Liberty's historical roots were adapted by a group of French political reformers to celebrate a set of beliefs and values that formed part of their own struggle in France to expand freedom and establish self-government.

The statue's original inspiration combined the longings of a particular people in a particular historical era with the symbols of human struggles generated over the course of history. Over time, Liberty transcended the horizons of both its creators and the people among whom it came to reside. It also exceeded the limits of its physical form. Ultimately, the Statue of Liberty became remarkably transformed into a universal symbol of extraordinary spiritual force.

European immigrants arriving in New York in the first half of the twentieth century glimpsed in Liberty's image the very image of their own longings and what they perceived to be the image of America itself. Yet, as China's Goddess of Democracy demonstrated in 1989, the Statue of Liberty's enduring significance is its representation of transcendent human ideals, bound neither to a particular people nor to a particular historical era. Liberty's foremost achievement, it can be argued, is its ability to renew itself in the face of historical change and respond to the needs and hopes of peoples everywhere, in every era.

Emma Lazarus, a young American writer, understood well people's need for symbols and ideals with which to elevate and ennoble life's spirit (fig. 1.4). Lazarus was born into a prominent Sephardic Jewish family in New York and devoted her career to literature, publishing a novel, a play, and two collections of poetry. Moved by the conditions of immigrants arriving in New York City, she visited a temporary immigrant shelter on Ward's Island in New York's East River in 1881 and became an advocate of refugee interests. Her celebrated poem honoring the Statue of Liberty, which she titled "The

14

Fig. 1.4. Emma Lazarus (1849–87). Lazarus's poem honoring the new Statue of Liberty, "The New Colossus," appeared in 1883 and reflected her commitment to immigrants from all nations. Sixteen years after Lazarus's death, a plaque with her poem was affixed to the statue's pedestal by Georgiana Schuyler, Lazarus's friend and an art patron. Wood engraving by T. Johnson. Photograph by W. Kurtz. Reprinted by permission of Library of Congress, Washington, D.C.

New Colossus," fixed for all time the statue's poetic and inspiring representation of the yearning for freedom, dignity, and self-government. Indeed, Liberty has become in the popular mind the guardian of these human ideals until such a day as they may triumph in the world. The Lazarus poem reads:

Not like the brazen giant of Greek fame,

With conquering limbs astride from land to land;

Here at our sea-washed, sunset gates shall stand

A mighty woman with a torch, whose flame

Is the imprisoned lightning, and her name

Mother of Exiles. From her beacon-hand

Glows world-wide welcome; her mild eyes command

The air-bridged harbor that twin cities frame.

"Keep, ancient lands, your storied pomp!" cries she

With silent lips. "Give me your tired, your poor,

Your huddled masses yearning to breathe free,

The wretched refuse of your teeming shore.

Send these, the homeless, tempest-tost to me.

I lift my lamp beside the golden door!"

BIBLIOGRAPHY

Blanchet, Christian, and Bertrand Dard. *Statue of Liberty: The First Hundred Years*. Translated from the French by Bernard A. Weisberger. New York: American Heritage Press, 1985.

Burns, Kenneth L. *The Statue of Liberty*. Transcript of the film *The Statue of Liberty*, produced and directed by Kenneth L. Burns and written by Bernard Weisberger and Geoffrey Ward. Walpole, N.H.: Florentine Films, 1985.

Cole, Donald B. *Handbook of American History*. New York: Harcourt, Brace, and World, 1968.

Garnett, John J. *The Statue of Liberty: Its History, Conception, Construction, and Inauguration*. New York: B. W. Dinsmore, 1886.

Handlin, Oscar. *Statue of Liberty*. New York: Newsweek Books, 1971.

Harris, Jonathan. *A Statue for America: The First 100 Years of the Statue of Liberty*. New York: Four Winds Press, 1985.

New York Public Library and Comité officiel Franco-Américain pour la célébration centenaire de la Statue de la Liberté, with Pierre Provoyeur and June Hargrove. *Liberty: The French-American Statue in Art and History*. New York: Harper and Row, 1986.

Pauli, Hertha, and E. B. Ashton. *I Lift My Lamp: The Way of a Symbol*. Port Washington, N.Y.: Ira J. Friedman, 1969.

Tocqueville, Alexis de. *Democracy in America*. Edited by J. P. Mayer and Max Lerner. Translated by George Lawrence. New York: Harper and Row, 1966.

Trachtenberg, Marvin. *The Statue of Liberty*. New York: Viking, 1976.

Williams, T. Harry, Richard N. Current, and Frank Freidel. *A History of the United States*. 2d ed. rev. New York: Alfred A. Knopf, 1964.

Zeldin, Theodore. *Intellect and Pride: France, 1848–1945*. Oxford and New York: Oxford University Press, 1980.

Liberty and Liberalism in Nineteenth-Century France and America

SEYMOUR DRESCHER

Perhaps one can best grasp the significance of liberty in the nineteenth century by beginning with France's most famous observer of America, Alexis de Tocqueville. Tocqueville and his traveling companion, Gustave de Beaumont, had been in the United States less than two months when they witnessed their first American national festival, in Albany, New York, on July 4, 1831.[1] The celebration made a deep and lasting impression. The solemn procession was unlike anything they had ever seen in France. Absent were the great military displays with which any self-respecting French provincial city would have garnished the festival—no dashing cavalry troops, no well-drilled infantry marching crisply by with its regimental flags and battle honors, all moving to the stirring sound of military bands. Absent was any assemblage of resplendently dressed officers of church and throne seated in stately carriages. In the capital of the largest state in the American Union, the military demeanor of the citizen militia struck the two French visitors as truly comic.

At the great ceremonial gathering that followed the parade the orchestral accompaniment consisted of a single flute vainly trying to make itself heard above the din of collective singing. The two

17

Frenchmen were, however, much more profoundly impressed by what the ceremonies contained than by what they lacked. The only people who rode in a carriage were a handful of surviving veterans. And the dominant participants in the great procession were the tradesmen and workingmen of Albany: the associations of butchers, of mechanics, of carpenters, of painters, of carmen, of volunteer firemen, of apprentices and typographers. The last group came by on a float that featured a printing press busily churning out copies of the Declaration of Independence for distribution among the on-lookers.

The ceremony itself centered around a reading of that docu-ment. It was not, noted the French observers, a theatrical perfor-mance: "There was in the reading of those promises of indepen-dence so well kept, in this return of an entire people toward the memories of its birth, in this union of the present generation to that which is no longer, sharing for the moment all its generous pas-sions, there was in all that something deeply felt and truly great."[2]

The unity of the population, not only around the idea of liber-ty but on a single documentary expression of that idea and the insti-tutions that articulated it, was what most astonished the newly ar-rived visitors (fig. 2.1). The contrast with their own experience was arresting. Tocqueville and Beaumont had left behind them a gov-ernment created less than a year before on the barricades of Paris, one that was being and was to be challenged again and again until it, too, finally fell before the barricades of 1848. Theirs was a govern-ment that had to ban public commemorations of its own birthday because they became the occasion for popular denunciations of promises betrayed.[3]

The contrast was indicative of the fate of liberalism in America and France during the first three-quarters of the nineteenth century.[4] The very term *liberal* was adopted by early-nineteenth-century French moderates who sought to preserve representative government against the return of old social privileges and autocratic government after the Bourbon Restoration of 1814.[5] Conversely, in America, the term *liberal* was rarely used to designate a political po-sition before the last quarter of the nineteenth century, because al-most all social groups employed the same libertarian vocabulary to express even the most divergent social values and goals.[6]

Such a dramatic divergence had not existed before the end of the eighteenth century. Both the Anglo-American and the French

Fig. 2.1. "Libertas Americana . . . 4 Juil. 1776." This bronze medal, designed by Benjamin Franklin in 1782, depicts American liberty as a female figure and associates the image with the date of American independence, July 4, 1776. During an 1871 visit to America, Liberty's creator, Frédéric-Auguste Bartoldi, sought ideas for a physical image of American liberty and studied medals and coins bearing female images. Photo R.M.N. Reprinted by permission of Musée National de la Coopération franco-américaine, Blérancourt.

libertarian traditions had emerged through a judicial mode of thought in which liberty was understood as a specific privilege, or right, that left a group or one of its members free to pursue specific activities or free from specific obligations. As this intellectual tradition evolved in the century and a half before the American and French revolutions, the rights designated by the concept of liberty began to be understood as inherent in all individuals. Political authority itself was increasingly conceived to be the result of the free surrender of a portion of those rights to ensure their more certain collective protection. The universalistic language of this natural rights theory had essentially ecumenical and egalitarian implications.

A great historical watershed occurred at the time of the two great Atlantic revolutions in 1776 and 1789. The American nation managed to strengthen both the egalitarian and the proprietary implications of early libertarian theory, literally driving opponents beyond the boundaries of the new nation. The liberal idea that took root in America was therefore an optimistic one, eminently suited to the small-producer capitalism of pre–Civil War America, with its preponderance of aspiring farmers, merchants, and artisans, producing for a rapidly expanding market.

It should be noted that although Tocqueville stressed the freedom to participate in the political process, nineteenth-century American society also rested on rapid economic expansion, which allowed great leeway for individual initiative. Adam Smith had given this economic aspect of liberalism its classic formulation in 1776. If all were allowed to act on the basis of self-interest in an unfettered market, both individuals and the society would achieve an optimal increase in material wealth. Resources would therefore be optimally allocated. This ideal was also well suited to the early Republic. Tocqueville was deeply impressed by America's relative freedom from bureaucratic control of the economy as of all other aspects of activity.

What made this individualistic ideal seem possible in antebellum America despite the impact of industrialization on large segments of the European working classes was the shared prognosis of Thomas Jefferson, James Madison, and others that America was and would remain exceptional. The liberal-republican language of "exceptionalism" dominated American political discourse in the mid-nineteenth century. This relatively democratic republican liberalism was so widespread in America by the 1830s that Tocqueville viewed it as almost universal.[7]

France, in the meantime, had a very different experience with its libertarian tradition after 1789. The nation passed first through the traumas of radical revolutionary dictatorship and state-sponsored terror and then, after a series of coups, through an authoritarian militaristic regime. The libertarian revolution seemed to be incapable of preventing its degeneration into a succession of anti-libertarian alternatives. Moreover, the returning opponents of the revolution, which included large segments of the secular and religious elite of the old regime, branded the libertarian ideology as one of the major sources of their collective misfortune. As a result, French defenders of liberty constituted only one faction of the political and ideological spectrum amid an array of monarchist and Bonapartist authoritarians, radical republicans, and socialists. For decades embattled French liberals devoted their energies to building walls around the concept of individual rights against the twin threats of arbitrary state power on the one hand and arbitrary revolutionary power on the other. The principal mechanism of defense consisted of confining political rights to a small proprietary elite, which could fend off the despotisms of the right and the left.[8]

How did liberals in each society view those in the other? For most French liberals and most articulate Americans, the egalitarian liberty of the United States was exceptional in a number of ways—in its political decentralization, its broad male suffrage, its demilitarized security, its sectarian pluralism, and its thinly occupied frontier.[9] Even those in the New World who were outside the American liberal consensus were considered exceptional, if they were considered at all. Either they were geographically outside the organized political system (like the Indians), or scarcely organized as a pressure group (like women), or denied full civil membership in the society (like slaves and free blacks). Furthermore, neither the blacks nor the Indians had counterparts in France.

In European terms, America's most significant exceptionality came not in the groups that were excluded but in those that were included—the farmers, artisans, and laborers of the Euro-American heritage. These were the classes that seemed to present the greatest threat to the French social order, and those to whom French liberals hesitated to accord political rights. When French observers considered flaws in American liberalism, they followed the American majority in focusing on slavery as the great pathology in the liberal consensus.[10] American and French liberals were therefore inclined to consider the American achievement exceptional in relation to a European world torn by class conflicts among aristocracies, middle classes, and urban workers.

Tocqueville's observations were also notable in that his long-run influence on French notions of liberty, drawn from America, was decisive in two respects. He was the first French liberal to emphasize that despite elements of exceptionality, America offered libertarian institutions and *moeurs* that were capable of being adapted to European circumstances. Second, and perhaps more important, Tocqueville convinced liberals of the following generation that the defensive strategy of protecting private liberty by confining political participation to a small electorate was doomed.[11]

Before 1848 French liberals had looked primarily to Great Britain, with its restricted suffrage, as the institutional model. The plebiscitary Caesarism of Louis Napoleon's Second Empire demonstrated that liberty would have to be founded on mass support, above all, the peasant proprietors and urban petite bourgeoisie who constituted the bulk of the French electorate. The post-Tocquevillian generation of liberals—Etienne Vacherot, Jules Simon, L. A. Prevost-Paradol, and Edouard-René Lefebvre de Laboulaye—therefore formulated a program of liberalization based on religious equality, broad national education, universal manhood suffrage, a free press, and a representative parliamentary system. Laboulaye's virtue as a popularizer of Tocqueville was to make this "American" program seem unthreatening and almost prosaic to the educated elite. Between the dangers of revolutionary or authoritarian dictatorship on the one side and majoritarian electoral tyranny on the other, the latter had to be risked to avert the far more antilibertarian effects of centralized despotism.

Half a century after Tocqueville's American visit, liberty appeared to have emerged triumphant on both sides of the Atlantic. In America, slavery, the most salient exception to the liberal ethos, had been abolished with the enthusiastic support of French liberals. The outcome of the Civil War was crucial for French liberals. Lincoln's reelection in 1864 was to Laboulaye "the salvation of the American republic and of the liberty which is of interest to the whole world. With the eradication of slavery America had matured." Immediately after Lincoln's assassination Laboulaye's students went en masse to express their condolences at the embassy, despite police intervention. A gold medal subscribed to by 40,000 French citizens was presented to Mary Todd Lincoln.[12] Finally, the victory of the North suggested to Laboulaye a larger, more appropriate gift to a "nation of liberals" from the people of France. That gift ultimately became, as we know, the Statue of Liberty.[13]

For their part, the French liberals had absorbed some valuable lessons from their own tumultuous conflicts. They had recognized the potential social conservatism of universal suffrage in 1848, in the "Liberal Empire" of the late 1860s, and in the elections of the 1870s, finally embedding parliamentary democracy in the democratic conservatism of France's small landholders.[14] The French liberal consensus was just strong enough to undermine the last Bourbon pretender when the latter failed to acquiesce in the supremacy of parliamentary government. The democratic republican analogy of America and France never seemed stronger than during the decade when the Statue of Liberty was under construction.

Just as the liberals were celebrating the convergence of Franco-

American institutions, liberalism was beginning to find itself engulfed in a new crisis. During the Gilded Age the American antebellum consensus about American exceptionalism weakened under the impact of rapid economic and urban concentration, worker and farmer protest, and the end of the American frontier. Among the industrial-financial elite, the harsher language of classical economics began to replace the old popular language of republican liberalism. Among workers, the theme of American exceptionalism began to be used as a radical weapon against the new industrialism in the name of more collectivist democratic institutions.[15]

The classic works of British economic individualism enjoyed an enormous revival, intensified by the antistatist Social Darwinism of Herbert Spencer. A new vision emerged of the individual as consumer, achieving his or her goals in the accumulation of market products. One strand of American liberalism accepted this development, arguing that economic efficiency was the principal superstructure of a liberal society. The state and the political activity that had once been the defining activity of liberty receded from its central position in this new liberalism.

On the other hand, among a growing class of propertyless workers in large-scale enterprise, the rhetoric of American exceptionalism began to be used as a radical weapon against the new "industrial" liberalism. The old abolitionist attack on slavery was extended to incorporate industrial "enslavement." The preferred solution was a society of workers' cooperatives, which would replace both the wage-system and large-scale capitalism. Thus the tensions between the market and the democratic republican ideal, which had coexisted uneasily since the eighteenth century, reemerged in a sharper confrontation.

In France the same economic tensions, which had long since attracted segments of the industrial working class to cooperative socialist schemes, drew them toward collectivist political parties and labor unions. Even more directly threatening to the republic, sympathy for authoritarian and radical solutions was revealed in a series of challenges to the new regime. As late as 1885, on the eve of the presentation of the Statue of Liberty, monarchists and Bonapartists captured more than two hundred seats in the French Chamber of Deputies. Many monarchists and clerical opponents of the regime referred to their republic not as the maiden of liberty but as *la geuse*—"the slut." Before the end of the century the Boulanger and

Dreyfus affairs reminded the French that their libertarian institutions were much more precariously rooted in their national traditions than were America's. Thus, if the contrast between liberalism in America and in France no longer seemed as stark at the end of the nineteenth century as it had appeared at the beginning, well into the next century the old French republican trilogy of liberty, equality, and fraternity could be treated with contempt by large segments of the political spectrum and swept aside for other political values.

The presentation of the Statue of Liberty by France to America in 1886 therefore came at an exceptionally tranquil moment in an otherwise turbulent history. It remains a symbol of a dynamic process rather than a monument to a settled consensus. The historical context surrounding the gift underlines the fact that the salience or centrality of any symbol is not fixed once and for all in memory or consciousness. But it is equally important to recall that the Atlantic liberal tradition has been flexible and durable enough to provide a source of inspiration for both those who wish to strengthen public life and those who wish to reinforce the libertarian individualism that we inherited from the nation-builders of the eighteenth and nineteenth centuries.

NOTES

1. George Wilson Pierson, *Tocqueville and Beaumont in America* (New York: Oxford University Press, 1938), 179–84.

2. Ibid., 183.

3. See André-Jean Tudesq, *Les Grands Notables en France (1840–1849)*, 2 vols. (Paris: Presses Universitaires de France, 1964), 1:516–57; David H. Pinkney, *The Decisive Years in France 1840–1847* (Princeton: Princeton University Press, 1986), 150–51; Robert L. Koepke, "The Failure of Parliamentary Government in France, 1840–1848," *European Studies Review* 9 (1979): 409–55. By "promises fulfilled," Tocqueville meant the drafting of the federal Constitution in 1787—that brief moment when America rose to "a climax of glory," found a remedy to its crisis of unity, and submitted to that remedy "voluntarily without its costing humanity a single tear or drop of blood"

(Alexis de Tocqueville, *Democracy in America*, ed. J. P. Mayer and Max Lerner, trans. George Lawrence [New York: Harper and Row, 1966], 102). Tocqueville was as impressed by the flexibility of the American Constitution as by any of its provisions. He contrasted France's immutable and discarded constitutions with the malleability of America's unique mode of judicial interpretation (ibid., 90–91, 697–98). He attributed the success of such an institution to the judicial habits that were so deeply ingrained in Americans (ibid., 252–53).

4. See Jean-Claude Lamberti, *Tocqueville et les deux democraties* (Paris: Presses Universitaires de France, 1983), 59–310; reprinted as *Tocqueville and the Two Democracies*, trans. Arthur Goldhammer (Cambridge, Mass.: Harvard University Press, 1989); Louis Hartz, *The Liberal Tradition in America* (New York: Harcourt Brace, 1955), 40–242.

5. Guido de Ruggiero, *The History of European Liberalism*, trans. R. G. Collingwood (Boston: Beacon Press, 1959), 158–210.

6. Samuel H. Beer, "Liberalism and the National Idea," in *Left, Right, and Center: Essays on Liberalism and Conservatism in the United States*, ed. Robert A. Goldwin (Chicago: Rand McNally, 1965), 142–69.

7. Tocqueville, *Democracy in America*, 1:54, 362–63.

8. Ruggiero, *History of European Liberalism*, chap. 2; Lamberti, *Les deux democraties*, 75–83. During the decade 1838–48 Tocqueville believed that the French, like the Americans, had definitively ended their era of turbulence and revolution. This concept was shattered by the French Revolution of 1848. See Seymour Drescher, "'Why Great Revolutions Will Become Rare': Tocqueville's Most Neglected Prognosis," *Journal of Modern History* 64 (September 1992): 429–54.

9. René Remond, *Les Etats-Unis devant l'opinion française, 1815–1852*, 2 vols. (Paris: A. Colin, 1962).

10. See Tocqueville, *Democracy in America*, 1 (pt. 2, chap. 10): 316–407.

11. Seymour Drescher, *Dilemmas of Democracy: Tocqueville and*

Modernization (Pittsburgh: University of Pittsburgh Press, 1968), chap. 2; Roger Solteau, *French Political Thought in the Nineteenth Century* (New York: Russel and Russel, 1959), chap. 9, sec. 1.

12. Serge Gavronsky, *The Liberal Opposition and the American Civil War* (New York: Humanities Press, 1968), chap. 14.

13. New York Public Library and Comité officiel Franco-Américain pour la célébration du centenaire de la Statue de la Liberté, with Pierre Provoyeur and June Hargrove, *Liberty: The French-American Statue in Art and History* (New York: Harper and Row, 1986).

14. Jacques Chastenet, *Histoire de la IIIe République*, 7 vols. (Paris: Hachette, 1952–63), vol. 2, *La République des républicains*.

15. David Montgomery, *Beyond Equality: Labor and the Radical Republicans, 1862–1872* (New York: Knopf, 1967); Dorothy Ross, "Socialism and American Liberalism: Academic Social Thought in the 1880's," in *Perspectives in American History*, vol. 11, ed. Donald Fleming (Cambridge, Mass.: Charles Warren Center for Studies in American History, 1977–78), 5–79; John L. Thomas, *Alternative America: Henry George, Edward Bellamy, Henry Demarest Lloyd, and the Adversary Tradition* (Cambridge, Mass.: Belknap Press, 1983).

The Universal Appeal of
the Statue of Liberty

CHRISTIAN BLANCHET

ne century after her construction, the Statue of Liberty is the monument, the quintessential symbol, to which the world turns whenever and wherever liberty is threatened or there is a cause to be defended. How did the Statue of Liberty earn this nearly universal following? What is the substance of her global appeal, and how does she evoke such strong feelings of identification?

Analysis of the several symbolic components of the statue will demonstrate that, as a product of the times, the statue responded directly to major issues and concerns prevailing at the end of the nineteenth century—both political and aesthetic. At the same time, the statue was infused by its creators with values far surpassing the era in which it was created, as well as the geographical boundaries of its new home. Originating as a French idea and then being placed in an American setting, the Statue of Liberty evolved into a universal symbol—indeed, a grand icon of the modern world.

HISTORICAL SETTING

To understand the appeal of the Statue of Liberty, one must first recall the historical and political setting in France in the second half of the nineteenth century—for that constitutes the statue's heritage.

In 1865, the French jurist Edouard-René Lefebvre de Laboulaye conceived the idea of offering a gift of friendship to the United States, commemorating the one hundredth birthday of American independence. France then was in the grip of an authoritarian regime known as the Second Empire (1852–70). In order to silence the republican and liberal forces of opposition, Emperor Napoleon III had imposed strict controls on society. The imperial police, however, were unable to quell the dissent of the people, who seized every opportunity to demonstrate against the oppressive regime.

Laboulaye was a professor of comparative law in the Collège de France, the author of several books on American democracy, and a great admirer of American constitutionalism. He was a leader in French liberal political circles. Inspired by American democracy, Laboulaye and his colleagues came to view the United States Constitution as an exemplary governing model for France.

Laboulaye's idea of a gift to the United States was intended as a symbol of friendship between France and the United States and as an expression of liberal opposition to the Second Empire. He relished the idea that one day liberal leadership would be restored to France. Yet Laboulaye realized that to ensure the stability of a future republican government, France would need allies. It could not count on its neighbors in Europe; for the most part, these were kingdoms and empires that constituted a permanent threat. That was why Laboulaye considered the United States a potential ally, and in doing so he manifested an extraordinary farsightedness.

Europe in 1865, it is worth recalling, was the center of the political world. Laboulaye, however, was one of the few intellectuals capable of envisioning future shifts in world power and the emergence of the power of the United States. He recognized that this new continent offered unforeseen and perhaps unlimited potential, which would eventually have to be reckoned with. Therefore, as the centennial of American independence drew near, Laboulaye decided it was "now or never"—time for a dramatic act that would renew the bonds of friendship established by the Marquis de Lafayette and

General George Washington a century earlier during the War of Independence. Furthermore, the American Civil War had just ended. In abolishing slavery, Lincoln had proved to the world that America truly was committed to the ideals proclaimed in its Declaration of Independence and Constitution.

In 1870 the Second Empire of Napoleon III had collapsed, and the emperor had capitulated in the Battle of Sedan. The Franco-Prussian War had been a disaster for France, which now faced what would be a turbulent period in its history, torn by the war, the violent and bloody repression of the Paris Commune, and the mounting internal political struggles. With the republic restored in 1870, power had shifted to the radical faction. The liberals, who stood at the edge of power, wanted to have a voice in the new government, but they had been shut out. Laboulaye's plan for a gift to the United States then resurfaced. The Statue of Liberty would be a compelling symbol, a striking demonstration of the bond between the two countries and a symbol of the spread of liberal ideas throughout the world—the ideas of liberty and democracy, above all. Liberty, as a new political force, satisfied a deep need for recognition by the French liberal opposition.

The Industrial Revolution in the second half of the nineteenth century also influenced the design and engineering of the Statue of Liberty. The industrializing nations of the West were inundated by a flow of new and powerful technological processes and inventions that fused visionary engineering designs with functional, practical applications. It was a period marked by scientific achievements. The development of industry, commerce, and world trade stimulated supply and demand. Railways, bridges, ports, and viaducts were built. Iron and reinforced concrete proliferated in the construction industry. The great engineers reigned—Gustave Eiffel, Ferdinand de Lesseps, John Augustus Roebling, to name a few. The Suez Canal was completed, and a new canal in Panama was being planned. Vast empires were established and territories conquered. The United States set out to tame its western regions, just as Europe was extending its reach by colonizing Africa and Asia. Major nations of the world celebrated their growing power by means of expositions that displayed new machines and industrial processes. World fairs became sites for friendly competition among the industrial powers.

THE STATUE'S ORIGINS

At a small dinner party in his home near Versailles on a summer evening in 1865, Laboulaye first raised the idea of a gift to the United States. A young sculptor, Frédéric-Auguste Bartholdi, was present that evening at the dinner. Having just received a commission to carve a bust of Laboulaye, Bartholdi had a keen interest in Laboulaye's idea of creating a monument in America to commemorate the centennial of American independence.

The idea for an American monument, however, was not immediately acted upon. At the time Bartholdi, a creator of monumental public art, was attracted to the prospect of building a majestic monument at the entrance to the Suez Canal in Egypt to celebrate the canal's opening and to symbolize progress among nations. He proposed a design to the Egyptian leader, Ismail Pasha, a statue and monument that would stand at the entrance to the canal and function as a lighthouse. It was to be called "L'Egypte apportant la lumière à l'Asie"—Egypt Bringing the Light to Asia—or "Progress." Bartholdi had a passion for grand art, and his dream was to create a new wonder of the world (fig. 3.1). The Egyptian project, however, never attracted financing, and it was abandoned in 1869. Following the restoration of republican government in France in 1870 and the revival of Laboulaye's idea of a gift to the United States, Bartholdi redirected his vision of a spectacular monument to human progress and liberty from the Suez Canal to New York Harbor.

Bartholdi's plans for a grand monument seemed to be tailor-made for the United States. During his first American journey in 1871, Bartholdi wrote to Laboulaye, "Everything is big here—even the peas, that is to say, things that I prefer to be small."[1] Bartholdi discerned in America a frenetic pace of activity, explosive growth, and a receptivity to new ideas, such as the one he was advancing for New York Harbor. One additional feature attracted him: America was a country, indeed a continent, that was uniquely propelled by an ideal—the ideal of liberty. The incarnation of that ideal would have to fit the scale of the country. Upon his return to France, Bartholdi became committed to creating a statue symbolizing human liberty that would be situated on Bedloe's Island at the entrance to New York Harbor.

Fig. 3.1. Suez lighthouse. Bartholdi sketched in watercolor a monument planned for the entrance to the Suez Canal in Egypt, 1867–69. Titled "Progress," or "Egypt Bringing the Light to Asia," the sketch is a forerunner of Bartholdi's design for the Statue of Liberty. Reproduction by Christian Kempf. Reprinted by permission of Musée Bartholdi, Colmar, France.

PUBLIC ART AND ITS POLITICAL MEANING

The political and ideological battles of the nineteenth century, waged by different groups and factions—among them nationalists, republicans, and supporters of military and authoritarian regimes—found expression in the arts and in the creation of artistic images in sculpture and painting. Large public monuments and freestanding statues became very popular in the late nineteenth century. Many of them were created to express support for a particular type of government, honor a military or political leader, commemorate a watershed political event, or symbolize a political principle or ideal to which large numbers of people aspired.

Champions of the republican ideals of liberty and equality looked upon public monuments as a vital means of communicating the values of a popular government to large numbers of people. Monuments were seen as important settings for raising popular awareness and winning public support for the republican side in the growing number of conflicts that the republican forces were waging against authoritarian, military, and dictatorial governments. The appeal of large-scale monuments was widely shared among republican-minded artists of the period. These artists, including Bartholdi, were convinced that republican art should be both vivid and grand in its dimensions and, further, that its setting should be spacious and highly visible in order to attract the largest number of ordinary people to its aesthetic qualities and symbolism.

The favor shown to grand monuments is evident, for example, in the words of Charles Blanc, director of the famous Parisian art academy, l'école nationale supérieure des Beaux-Arts. Speaking at a lighthouse design competition in 1878, Blanc stated: "When a figure is constructed at the mouth of an ocean passageway, overlooking the sea, to be visible from afar, both by navigators and those who dwell on the shore, it is vital that it be a solid and unbroken mass. In other words, uncluttered, without detached pieces, without holes . . . For a statue to be easily read at a distance from which it will be perceived, it is essential that it have simple flowing lines and a smooth silhouette, long and perfectly intelligible. As to the form, the smaller planes should melt into the larger overall planes."[2]

THE STATUE'S SYMBOLISM

All sides to these political struggles, typically, invoked for the purposes of artistic representation the myths, symbols, and art of antiquity as sources of inspiration. Classical Greek and Roman art, in particular, became the basis for the monumental art that the French and Germans were seeking to create in the late nineteenth century.

Among the most prominent of the ancient symbols was the Goddess of Liberty, which had been glorified as early as the third century B.C. in the Roman Republic. Numerous statues and other public monuments were created in late-nineteenth-century Germany and France, consisting in many cases of a robed, standing female figure holding a scepter or staff. These figures usually were adorned by a cap, bonnet, or helmet and were surrounded by other symbolic representations, such as a cat, a piece of chain, or a broken jug.

In the United States at the time, another type of female figure,

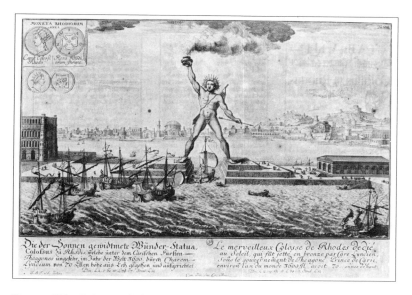

Fig. 3.2. "The Colossus of Rhodes," an engraving from J. B. Fischer von Erlach, in *Entwurf einer historischen Architektur*, Leipzig, c. 1721. Said to have been a bronze statue of the ancient Greek sun-god Helios, the Colossus of Rhodes was designed by Chares of Lindos. It exceeded 100 feet in height and stood at the harbor entrance of the island of Rhodes. Its design was a major influence on Bartholdi's design for Liberty. Reprinted by permission of l'école national supérieure des Beaux-Arts, Paris.

which came to be known as Columbia, also was seen adorning public monuments. Columbia in some cases was depicted as wearing an American Indian headdress in place of a bonnet or cap. The affinity between Columbia and classical female figures representing liberty is very striking. Both types of figures were found on the coins of the period in Europe and in the United States.

Frédéric-Auguste Bartholdi, the creator of the Statue of Liberty, was strongly influenced by classical Greek and Roman models, and in his work he combined this classical inspiration with his own deeply held belief in the compelling visual quality of colossal monuments (fig. 3.2).

Bartholdi's design strove to merge aesthetic qualities with the political and philosophical values that prevailed then. Liberty's gesture, her forward-moving stride and her upraised arm holding the torch, depicts a highly dynamic and powerful figure that conveys an arresting aesthetic appeal of its very own. Yet what constitutes, ultimately, the unique power and the universal appeal of the Statue of Liberty is the principle of human liberty on which she rests, her personification of the abstract ideal of liberty. Victor Hugo, France's most celebrated literary figure and republican leader, proclaimed, after paying a visit to the statue as it stood in a Paris neighborhood before being shipped to the United States: "A statue is all and nothing at all. It is nothing in and of itself, yet it is everything when it embodies an idea."[3]

Liberty is, of course, the idea behind the Statue of Liberty. But what notion of liberty did the creators have in mind?

The Goddess of Liberty in ancient times signified a personal condition or attribute rather than a social and political one. Liberty was the condition of an individual who was not enslaved or owned by another person. In modern times, however, the meaning of liberty became broader. Personal freedom was joined by a broader range of public freedoms, such as the right to speak freely or to worship according to the religion of one's choice. Other public and political liberties included the right to vote, to criticize and dissent from political decisions, and to participate in choosing the form of government under which one lives. Furthermore, by the late nineteenth century slavery had been abolished in many countries, including the United States. The ancient Roman idea of liberty as personal freedom from enslavement was no longer relevant.

The concept of liberty that the Statue of Liberty was intended to represent, according to its creators, Laboulaye and Bartholdi, bore little relationship to another well-known notion of freedom that existed in France and was depicted in the art of the period. One of the most famous paintings of the nineteenth century is an 1830 canvas by the French artist Eugène Delacroix (1798–1863), titled *La Liberté guidant le peuple* (Liberty Leading the People). The painting, which commemorates the 1830 July Revolution that overthrew the reactionary King Charles X, shows a militant female figure, wearing a Phrygian cap, charging over the bodies of the dead who fought and were killed in the revolution. The figure, holding in one arm the tricolor flag of France and carrying in the other arm a riflelike weapon, is leading an angry band of followers. Delacroix's idea of liberty is the liberty of violent revolution, the idea that freedom lies

Fig. 3.3. *La Liberté guidant le peuple* (Liberty Leading the People). Eugène Delacroix's 1830 painting became one of the most celebrated symbols of liberty and popular revolution in France. Photo R.M.N. Reprinted by permission of Musée du Louvre, Paris.

in uprooting tyranny, tyrannical rulers, and tradition-bound institutions (fig. 3.3).

Laboulaye in 1876 examined the difference between the idea of liberty in the Statue of Liberty and the idea of revolutionary liberty: "The statue is well named; she is truly Liberty, but American Liberty. She is not Liberty with a red cap on her head and a pike in her hand, stepping over corpses. Ours, in one hand holds the torch,— no, not the torch that sets afire, but the flambeau, the candle-flame that enlightens. In her other, she holds the tablets of the Law. . . . This statue, symbol of liberty, tells us . . . that Liberty lives only through Truth and Justice, Light and Law. This is the Liberty that we desire."[4]

The notion of liberty depicted by the statue is the aspect of freedom that is bound up in law and legal process. The statue communicates a sense of universal freedom and dignity that all human beings ought to enjoy, irrespective of social status and wealth. This image of freedom is linked to notions of equality, fairness, due process, and equal treatment under the law. Its substance is the opposite of notions of partisanship, factionalism, and revolutionary strife.

One other aspect has to be cited in any discussion of the symbolism of the Statue of Liberty and its representation of the ideal of liberty. Several of the statue's important features, such as the torch, the book of the law, and the radiating crown, derive from symbols associated with a social movement known as freemasonry. Freemasons were united by their belief in a supreme being, in universal brotherhood, and in the idea of enlightenment and the spread of truth as the basis for a just and free society. Organized in lodges throughout England and Europe, freemasonry spread to the American colonies in the eighteenth century. The Freemasons in France were identified with liberal and pro-American politics. Bartholdi, a member of the Freemason lodge known as the Lodge of Alsace-Lorraine, incorporated in the statue a number of images of freemasonry that resonated with the secular ideas of equality and liberty that were so prominent in France. His name for the statue, for example, Liberty Enlightening the World, reflected a major theme of Freemason thought.

By anchoring the statue's image of liberty in law and in universally agreed-upon legal processes of government, Laboulaye and Bartholdi avoided the possibility that the statue would become a parochial symbol of one nation's successful struggle for freedom or a glorification of a singular nationhood and nationalism. Liberty, on the contrary, became a universal symbol for all human beings who aspired to freedom.

Albert LeFaivre, France's consul general in New York, offered these remarks at the unveiling of the Statue of Liberty in New York Harbor on October 28, 1886: "Liberty is not only a common doctrine for us, the French and American people; it is a family tie. Because it is from this alliance between two nations that her expansive strength and brilliant rays issue forth, spanning the entire world. . . . This statue speaks to all mankind, not just to the people of these two republics, but to the myriad of people on this earth who work, dream and look towards her light."[5]

The Statue of Liberty that Bartholdi finally created brought together in a remarkable way the main intellectual and aesthetic currents that had first taken shape at Laboulaye's dinner party in 1865. It was, indeed, a public monument and a gift of the French people to the American people, commemorating the friendship and alliance of the two nations. It was also a colossal statue that would capture the imagination of peoples throughout the world. Finally, the statue symbolized the ascendancy of liberty, enlightenment, and progress, reflecting timeless and universal aspirations.

The day after the Statue of Liberty's inauguration and unveiling in 1886, Liberty already had become far more than a symbol of friendship between France and the United States. She had become the most powerful modern symbol of the longings of human beings everywhere for freedom, dignity, and well-being.

NOTES

1. Letter from Bartholdi to Laboulaye, dated July 15, 1871, Archives Laboulaye and Musée Bartholdi, Colmar, France.

2. Article signed by Charles Blanc, published in the newspaper *Le Temps*, dated March 27, 1878, Bibliotheque Nationale, Paris, and Archives of the Conservatoire Nationale des Arts et Métiers (CNAM)—Fonds Bartholdi.

3. Letter from Victor Hugo to Bartholdi, dated May 13, 1885. The precise sentence is "La forme au statuaire est tout, et ce n'est rien. Ce n'est rien dans l'esprit; c'est tout avec l'idée."

4. Laboulaye's speech at the opera of Paris, April 25, 1876, published "in extenso" in the newspaper *L'Evenement*, dated May 1, 1876, Bibliotheque Nationale, Paris, and Archives CNAM—Fonds Bartholdi.

5. Speech of Albert LeFaivre on October 28, 1886, published in the *Evening Star*, dated November 5, 1886, Archives CNAM—Fonds Bartholdi in Paris and the New York Public Library.

The Lady and the Huddled Masses

The Statue of Liberty as a Symbol of Immigration

RUDOLPH J. VECOLI

he Statue of Liberty stands in the harbor of New York City, a massive, dull, and ungainly sculpture. Yet it has become a powerful global symbol, ubiquitous, inescapable, protean, pressed into the service of a potpourri of causes, exploited for political commentary, advertising, and irreverent satire. Most recently, it served as the model for the ill-fated Goddess of Democracy built in Beijing's Tiananmen Square.[1]

While the statue has universal appeal, it occupies a special place in American life, though endowed with multiple meanings by its acolytes. Known variously as Liberty Enlightening the World, the Lady with the Torch, and the Goddess of Liberty, the statue has symbolized republican ideals, human freedom, and Franco-American friendship. In time it came to be the icon personifying the United States of America itself, succeeding its predecessors, Uncle Sam and Miss Columbia.[2]

The dominant interpretation during the centennial observances, however, was that of Mother of Exiles, the maternal presence that had welcomed millions of immigrants. It was not an accident that the chairman of the Statue of Liberty–Ellis Island Centennial Commission and Foundation was Lee Iacocca, whose parents had sailed past the statue upon their arrival from Italy. For Iacocca, the Lady with the Torch was an "enduring symbol of hope" for the immigrants and for their descendants[3]—not at all what its creators had intended it to represent. As conceptualized by Edouard-René Lefebvre de Laboulaye, French legal scholar and historian, and executed by Alsatian sculptor Frédéric-Auguste Bartholdi, the monument was to be a centennial gift from the French people, representing republican ideals and Franco-American amity. Bartholdi gave it the grandiose name Liberty Enlightening the World.[4]

Although the money for the statue was raised by popular subscription in France, the sluggish campaign in the United States to finance the pedestal threatened the success of the entire enterprise. In response to an appeal for literary manuscripts to be auctioned off for the pedestal fund, poet Emma Lazarus in 1883 wrote her sonnet "The New Colossus." It was she who named the statue Mother of Exiles and whose lines, spoken by the statue, created the classic stereotype of the immigrants: "Give me your tired, your poor,/Your huddled masses yearning to breathe free,/The wretched refuse of your teeming shore./Send these, the homeless, tempest-tost to me./I lift my lamp beside the golden door."[5]

Since New York was the major port of entry for the ever-increasing influx of Europeans, this perception of the relationship between the statue standing in the middle of the harbor and the arriving shiploads of immigrants was too obvious to be missed. Poets other than Lazarus also made the connection. John Boyle O'Reilly, the Irish Fenian writer, versified: "And hither, ye weary ones and breathless,/searching the seas for a kindly shore,/I am Liberty! patient, deathless,/set by Love at the Nation's door!"[6] A journalist writing in the *New York Evening Telegram* a full decade before the statue's dedication had noted: "Standing upon the threshold of New York, which is the doorway of the Union, she will seem to offer the freedom of the New World to the thousands who flock to us from the Old . . . that freedom which gathers the downtrodden and oppressed to her bosom, even as a hen gathers her chicken [*sic!*] under her wings."

But it was the immigrants themselves who imposed their own meaning on the Lady with the Torch. When Joseph Pulitzer, publisher of the *New York World* and himself a Hungarian immigrant, launched his successful campaign for the pedestal fund, the foreign-born were among the first to respond. One accompanied his contribution with the comment "I would send you more if I could, as I know how to appreciate liberty, because I am a Jew and emigrated from Russia to this city a few years ago." The Cuban revolutionary José Martí, who reported on the unveiling of the statue, noted: "Irishmen, Poles, Italians, Czechs, Germans freed from tyranny or want—all hail the monument of Liberty because to them it seems to incarnate their own uplifting."[7]

To the millions of arriving immigrants, beset by anxieties and fears as they anticipated their encounter with this strange land, the statue appeared to open its arms in a maternal embrace. It was they who took it to their hearts and transformed Bartholdi's colossus into the Mother of the Immigrants.[8] Immigrant memories of the first sighting of the statue are often rapturous in their evocation of deeply felt emotions. An elderly Ukrainian recently recalled, "When you see that Liberty Statue, when you see that open hand, it's the greatest feeling. It's like going to heaven and God accepts you."[9]

Edward Corsi, who came as a boy with his family from Abruzzi and was to become the commissioner at Ellis Island, remembered: "Mothers and fathers lifted up the babies so that they too could see, off to the left, the Statue of Liberty. I looked at that statue with a sense of bewilderment, half doubting its reality. Looming shadowy through the mist, it brought silence to the decks of the 'Florida.' This symbol of America—this enormous expression of what we had all been taught was the inner meaning of this country we were coming to—inspired awe in the hopeful immigrants."[10]

Edward A. Steiner, an immigrant who became a professor, captured the moment: "The steerage is still mute. . . . Slowly the ship glides into the harbor, and when it passes under the shadow of the Statue of Liberty, the silence is broken, and a thousand hands are outstretched in greeting to this new divinity to whose keeping they now entrust themselves."[11]

Indeed, a religious aura enveloped the attitude of reverence with which the immigrants regarded the statue. For Catholic peasants, what could she possibly have been but a madonna? An Italian woman many years in the United States kept on her bureau a miniature of Santa Liberata (Statue of Liberty), next to the Madonna of Montevergine.[12] When postal workers in Hungary sent a petition

Fig. 4.1. A Hungarian painting depicting women in peasant costume praising the Statue of Liberty. The inscription *"Veni Libertas"* at the bottom "Hail Liberty." This image accompanied a petition sent in March 1932 to President Herbert Hoover by a group of Hungarian postal workers. Reprinted by permission of National Archives, Washington, D.C.

to President Herbert Hoover, a beautiful painting depicting peasant women in an attitude of adoration toward the Statue of Liberty bearing the inscription *Veni Libertas* (Hail Liberty) adorned the cover (fig. 4.1).[13]

The symbolism of Liberty welcoming the newcomers quickly became fixed in American iconography. Illustrations in popular magazines portrayed steerage passengers in peasant garb saluting the statue (fig. 4.2).[14] The text accompanying such a sketch of 1892 reads: "Entering a New World: Bartholdi's great statue of liberty in New York harbour has a serious meaning for the many shiploads of expatriated Russian Jews to whom it seems to offer a welcoming hand."[15] The symbolic linkage of the statue with emigration was disseminated throughout Europe by emigrant guides of transatlantic shipping lines.[16] The statue was early incorporated into the logos of ethnic fraternal organizations, such as *landsmanshaften*, as though they had placed themselves under its protection (fig. 4.3).[17]

The statue was also the preferred symbol for manuals published by public authorities and by civic organizations devoted to

Fig. 4.2. "Welcome to the Land of Freedom—An Ocean Steamer Passing the Statue of Liberty: Scene on the Steerage Deck." This sketch is perhaps the earliest portrayal of arriving immigrants on the deck of a ship, viewing the Statue of Liberty with awe and reverence. From *Frank Leslie's Weekly*, July 2, 1887.

Fig. 4.3. Title page of the char-
ter and by-laws of an immigrant benevolent society. Immigrants from many countries,
upon arriving in the United
States, formed societies for
mutual assistance and sociabili-
ty. Among Jewish immigrants
from Eastern Europe these
groups were called *landsmanshaften*. The Bogopoler Unter-
stutzungs Verein was formed
in New York City in 1893.
Originally printed by Essex
Press of New York. Repro-
duced by permission of Yivo
Institute for Jewish Research,
New York City.

the teaching of citizenship and English.[18] Pageants in which a child
robed as the Statue of Liberty "welcomed" other children dressed in
ethnic costumes were performed in the public schools (fig. 4.4).[19]
By the early twentieth century, the statue and immigration had become inextricably intertwined in the minds of Americans as well as
those of immigrants.

The Statue of Liberty, however, was not always a benign or un-
equivocal oracle with respect to questions of immigration policy.
The closing decades of the nineteenth century were a time of increasing nativism and agitation for immigration restriction.[20] Indeed, the irony that the "Golden Door" was being shut against certain persons at the same time that the Goddess of Liberty was rising
in New York Harbor was not lost on contemporaries. In 1882 the
first broad federal immigration law excluded convicts, lunatics, id-
iots, and paupers. That same year, the Chinese Exclusion Act of
1882 barred entry to Chinese laborers and denied citizenship to
Chinese (fig. 4.5).

Fig. 4.4. Schoolchildren in New York City's P.S. 188, c. 1910, performing a pageant celebrating American liberty. Children in native costumes express gratitude toward the Lady with the Torch for her welcome to America. Such pageants were important means of socialization. Source: Collection of Stephan F. Brumberg.

In "A Chinese View of the Statue of Liberty," published in 1885, Saum Song Bo declared:

> The word liberty makes me think of the fact that this country is the land of liberty for men of all nations except the Chinese. I consider it as an insult to us Chinese to call on us to contribute toward building in this land a pedestal for a statue of Liberty. That statue represents Liberty holding a torch which lights the passage of those of all nations who come into this country. But are the Chinese allowed to come? As for the Chinese who are here, are they allowed to enjoy liberty as men of all other nationalities enjoy it? Are they allowed to go about everywhere free from the insults, abuse, assaults, wrongs and injuries from which men of other nationalities are free? . . . Whether this statute against the Chinese [the 1882 Chinese Exclusion Act] or the statue to Liberty will be the more lasting monument to tell future ages of the liberty and greatness of this country will be known only to future generations.[21]

Fig. 4.5. "Every Dog (No Distinction of Color) Has His Day." This cartoon, published by Harper and Brothers in 1879, depicts growing public hostility toward immigrants and persons of different ethnic and racial backgrounds. A Native American Indian is seen talking with an American of Chinese descent. Reprinted by permission of National Park Service, Statue of Liberty National Monument.

Six months before the inauguration of the statue, the explosion of a bomb in Chicago's Haymarket Square following a labor conflict touched off "a torrent of nationalist hysteria." The press attributed the act to "long-haired, wild-eyed, atheistic, reckless foreign wretches" and demanded vengeance. Seven anarchists, six of them immigrants, were sentenced to death, and four were actually hanged, not for throwing the bomb but for advocating their beliefs.[22] Chauncey M. Depew, president of the New York Central Railroad and orator of the day at the unveiling of the statue, clearly had them in mind when he qualified the open invitation that had been extended by Emma Lazarus: "The rays from this beacon, lighting this gateway to the continent, will welcome the poor and the persecuted with the hope and promise of homes and citizenship. It will teach them that there is room and brotherhood for all who will support our institutions and aid in our development; but *those who come to disturb our peace and dethrone our laws are aliens and enemies forever.*"[23]

The Haymarket Riot, which triggered the first major Red Scare in the United States, fixed the association of foreigners and radicalism in the public mind. This national phobia resulted in legislation that denied admission to and provided for the deportation (and even denaturalization) of anarchists and others who were thought to pose a threat to the existing order.[24] In a Thomas Nast cartoon of 1889, it is the stereotypical pugnacious Irishman, brandishing his shillelagh at the statue, who is "agin the Government."[25]

A young woman arriving from czarist Russia in 1886 was enraptured by her first sight of the Statue of Liberty: "Ah, there she was, the symbol of hope, of freedom, of opportunity! She held her torch high to light the way to the free country, the asylum for the oppressed of all lands. We, too . . . would find a place in the generous heart of America." Soon disillusioned with American capitalism, Emma Goldman became a militant leader of radical causes. In 1919, she and five hundred others were deported to the Soviet Union on the S.S. *Buford* (known as the Red Ark). Goldman recalled her departure: "Through the port-hole I could see the great city receding into the distance, its sky-line of buildings traceable by their rearing heads. It was my beloved city, the metropolis of the New World. It was America, indeed, America repeating the terrible scenes of tsarist Russia! I glanced up—the Statue of Liberty!"[26]

The Mother of Exiles now recognized as her children only

Fig. 4.6. Cartoon showing European garbage ships dumping their refuse—immigrants—at the feet of the Statue of Liberty, who expresses chagrin and disgust. Says Liberty: "If you're going to turn this island into a garbage dump, I'm going back to France." Cartoons such as this one depicting bigotry toward newcomers, which appeared in *Judge* on March 22, 1890, were common in American periodicals of the period. Reprinted by permission of National Park Service, Statue of Liberty National Monument.

those who could pass the litmus test of ideological purity. The Statue of Liberty was on occasion pressed into service in the cause of immigration restriction. The 1890s witnessed a sharp decline in the number of arrivals from the peak years of the 1880s, yet the economic crisis and social unrest of that decade inspired an intensified antiimmigrant sentiment. *Judge*, which catered to the bigotry of its middle-class readers with scurrilous cartoons of Irish, Negroes, and Jews, depicted the statue in 1890 as "the future emigrant lodging house."[27] More vicious was a cartoon in which Liberty pulls up her robe disdainfully as European garbage ships dump refuse at her feet (a literal interpretation of Lazarus's "wretched refuse") (fig. 4.6).[28]

Equally contemptuous was a cartoon of 1892 in which Liberty holds her nose with one hand while in the other she clutches a bottle of carbolic acid to kill the stench of the "dregs of Europe."[29]

Eastern European Jews, Italians, and Slavs were arriving in increasing numbers, and the mounting hostility toward immigrants was directed particularly at them. The Immigration Restriction League, formed in 1894 by a group of Boston Brahmins, for example, agitated for a literacy test, which was intended to limit the influx of southern and eastern Europeans. Thomas Bailey Aldrich, New England patrician and editor of the *Atlantic Monthly*, voiced these fears of the "wild, motley throng" in his poem "Unguarded Gates": "O Liberty, white Goddess! is it well/to leave the gates unguarded? On thy breast/fold Sorrow's children, soothe the hurts of fate,/lift the down-trodden, but with hand of steel/stay those who to thy scared portals come/to waste the gifts of freedom. Have a care lest from thy brow the clustered stars be torn and trampled in the dust."[30]

Within the short span of a decade, the statue had been transformed from welcoming Mother of Exiles to Guardian of the Gates against the invading hordes.

With the dawning of a new century, a postcard portrays Uncle Sam drawing back the flag to introduce Miss Liberty,[31] who was soon to replace him as the national symbol. Economic prosperity had returned, and the decrepit Spanish empire had been crushed. The triumphal mood of the country was captured in another postcard, which, with cannons blazing about the statue, proclaims "Liberty for All." Americans could afford to be more relaxed about immigration, despite its unprecedented heights in the first decade of the twentieth century, when in some years the number of arrivals exceeded a million.

The writer O. Henry expressed the more tolerant attitude in a vignette that took the form of a dialogue between the Statue of Liberty and the statue of Diana situated atop the Madison Square Garden Tower. The "Lady Higher Up," as O. Henry styled Liberty, speaks in an Irish brogue as she explains to Diana her mission: "If ye wasn't so light-headed and giddy ye'd know that I was made by a Dago [author's note: it was a common error to assume that Bartholdi was Italian] and presented on behalf of the French government for the purpose of welcomin' Irish immigrants to the Dutch city of New York." Liberty goes on to complain: "'Tis weary work . . . disseminatin' the science of liberty in New York Bay. Sometimes when I take a peep down at Ellis Island and see the gang of immigrants I'm supposed to light up, 'tis tempted I am to blow out the gas and let the coroner write out their naturalization papers."

But Diana reassures "Aunt Liberty": "That's a pretty sick-looking bunch of liberty chasers they dump down at your end of it; but they don't all stay that way. Every little while up here I see guys signing checks and voting the right ticket, and encouraging the arts and taking a bath every morning, that was shoved ashore by a dock labourer born in the United States who never earned over forty dollars a month."[32]

Between 1892 and 1924, some twenty million "liberty chasers" entered the United States, more than 70 percent of them through the port of New York. The statue's proximity to Ellis Island placed the newcomers almost literally "in the shadow of Liberty" while they anxiously awaited the outcome of their fate. A photograph of an immigrant family on Ellis Island looking across the bay at the statue conveys a sense of that mixture of anticipation and apprehension (fig. 4.7).[33]

More than a third of the immigrants during these years returned to their homelands, after a shorter or longer sojourn in America. Some, having realized their modest ambitions, repatriated to enjoy their hard-earned gains. Others, broken in body or spirit, fled this land. Unlike the abundant testimony of the arriving immigrants, we have few accounts of those who viewed the statue from the stern of a departing vessel. The poet Emanuel Carnevali, ill and disillusioned, in his bitter farewell, "The Return," did not mention Liberty. For him, "the naive skyscrapers, votive candles/at the head of supine Manhattan" were the monuments of "tremendously laborious America,/builder of mechanical cities."[34]

Arriving in 1916, Aleksandra Kollontai, Russian feminist and Bolshevik, did not spy the fog-enshrouded statue ("that symbol which once caused the hearts of our European fathers and grandfathers to beat with triumphant happiness and exultation"). She first saw Liberty from the steamer on which she sailed back to the Old World:

> Is that the Statue of Liberty? So tiny, lost in the noise of the harbour and framed against the soaring skyscrapers of the Wall Street banks. Was this powerless, tiny figure shrinking before the all-

Fig. 4.7. A newly arrived immigrant family on Ellis Island,
gazing across the bay at the
Statue of Liberty. This first
view of the statue remained
vividly embedded in the memories of millions of people who
entered the United States
through the port of New York.
Photograph by Richard H.
Schneider. Reprinted by permission of Library of Congress,
Washington, D.C.

powerful gigantic skyscrapers, those guardians of financial deals,
the Statue of Liberty we had pictured to ourselves? . . . It is these
solid walls of stone, the safe refuge of the kings of American capital, which now more completely express the "spirit" that reigns
over the continent of Columbus than the pitiful, shrunken, green
statue that seems to be embarrassed.[35]

If Kollontai had seen the statue later that year after it received a
bath and a new lighting system for its thirtieth birthday, she might
have been more favorably impressed. Although a lighthouse in
name, the statue had for decades stood in the harbor with only a
dim beacon flickering in the night (and on occasion, the torch was
extinguished for lack of funds). On December 2, 1916, President
Woodrow Wilson gave the signal from the presidential yacht for the
floodlight illumination. A *New York Times* reporter captured the
event: "A rocket went up from the Mayflower, a rocket answered
from Bedlow's Island and a moment later, as if touched by a magic
hand, the great statue sprang into view, the pedestal a beautiful
brown and Liberty a great green figure."[36]

Parades, ceremonies, and a banquet at the Waldorf marked the occasion. In his remarks, President Wilson called for rededication to the ideal of liberty and alluded to "the thrill that much [*sic*] come into some hopeful heart as for the first time an immigrant sees that statue and thinks he knows what it means." Then the president waxed philosophical: "I wonder if, after he lands, he finds the spirit of liberty truly represented by us? I wonder if we are worthy of that symbol; I wonder if we are sufficiently stirred by the history of it, by the history of what it means?"[37]

Some immigrants had already passed judgment on those questions. During the Red Scare of 1908, President Theodore Roosevelt had ordered anarchist publications barred from the mails and alien anarchists deported. One manifesto, the Italian-American publication *Il Gruppo La Questione Sociale*, lamented that the country "which is proud of the gigantic monument which rises at the mouth of the Hudson, on the one hand guarantees the liberty to write our thoughts, while on the other it strangles our voice and breaks our pen. Under the skin of the Statue of Liberty is hidden, insidious and wicked, St. Ignatius Loyola."[38] Ludovico Caminita, editor of *La Questione Sociale* of Paterson, New Jersey, reflected: "Before that monument the emigrant forgets the distant patria and with it the sorrows experienced; he opens his heart to the sweetest hopes and he is impatient to touch and kiss the promised land. . . . Oh, the hard reality of things! What bitter disillusionment future experience brings to the ingenuous immigrant!"[39]

The presidential order also inspired a cartoon, "Metamorfosi," in which the statue is transformed into a helmeted Theodore Roosevelt, holding a billy club aloft in one hand and a rifle in the other, while the caption contrasts the constitutional guarantee of freedom of speech and press with the legislation punishing any person who by speech or writing promotes or encourages hostility or opposition to any and all government (fig. 4.8).[40]

An answer was also given to Wilson's questions by Giuseppe Iannarelli, an organizer for the Workers' International Industrial Union, speaking in Niagara Falls in June 1917: "When the Italians enter this country they see the Statue of Liberty and they breathe freely thinking to themselves that they have at last left the autocratic government and are in the land of the free. Shortly after their arrival they realize their mistake, they become slaves to the capitalists who own them soul and body."[41]

Fig. 4.8. "Metamorfosi." One of the first cartoons representing an immigrant viewpoint that uses the Statue of Liberty to deliver a politically critical statement to the United States government regarding restrictive immigration policy. This depiction was inspired by President Theodore Roosevelt's suppression of the anarchist movement, particularly among Italian-Americans. The cartoon appeared in *L'Internazionale* on January 15, 1909. Source: Collection of Rudolph J. Vecoli.

The illumination of the statue took place in the midst of the Preparedness Campaign, which was designed to ready the American people militarily and psychologically for war. Within five months, the United States had entered World War I on the side of France, and the statue, the symbol of the ancient Franco-American alliance, was conscripted into national service. Secretary of the Treasury William G. McAdoo hit upon the idea of "Liberty Bonds" to finance the war effort, and Miss Liberty became the principal motif of patriotic propaganda.[42] Since more than a third of the American population was composed of immigrants and their children, particular stress was placed on the debt of gratitude and loyalty owed by the foreign-born to America. Posters urging them to buy Liberty Bonds or to conserve food portrayed shipboard immigrants viewing the statue, with such captions as "Remember Your First Thrill of American Liberty" or "You came here seeking Freedom You must now help preserve it" (fig. 4.9).[43]

World War I fostered the "One hundred Per Cent Americanization" crusade, which increased pressures upon the foreign-born

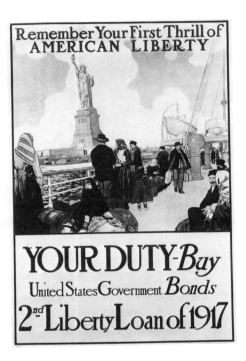

Fig. 4.9. "Remember Your First Thrill of American Liberty." During World War I, the Statue of Liberty became the dominant symbol invoked in government campaigns to finance the war effort. This poster was part of a second Liberty Loan campaign, appealing to recent immigrants to show their gratitude by purchasing war bonds. Reprinted by permission of Library of Congress, Washington, D.C.

to assimilate and become citizens. It also triggered an ugly nativism, which expressed itself in public and vigilante action against "hyphenates," especially German Americans and radicals.[44] The Bolshevik Revolution of November 1917 precipitated a Red Scare that continued into the postwar years. During this period, cartoons such as one of Miss Liberty being assailed by foreign-looking revolutionaries with bombs who were identified as "Bolsheviks" and stood in contrast to sympathetic portraits of immigrants in the propaganda posters.[45] Radicals of every stripe, particularly foreigners, were beaten, jailed, and deported. The deportation in 1919 of more than five hundred "Bolsheviks" to the Soviet Union inspired a cartoon by Boardman Robinson: smoke from the departing S.S. *Buford* (the Red Ark) blinds the Statue of Liberty.[46]

Carlo Tresca, an Italian-born radical, devoted the May 1920 issue of New York–based *Guardia Rossa* to "The White Terror in America." Reflecting on the injustice and inhumanity of lynchings, police brutality, and denial of free speech, Tresca confessed his profound disillusionment with the United States:

> When the ship which transported us to America passed before the historic, colossal Statue of Liberty there was a joyous rush to the side; all eyes were fixed on that torch of light, seeking to penetrate the breast of that woman, symbolizing the most dear of human aspirations, *La Liberta*, to see if there was a heart within which beat for all of the political refugees, for all of the slaves of capital, for the disinherited of the world. . . . Now I am disillusioned. . . . Perhaps I will pass again, still a pilgrim of the faith, before that statue. Like so many of my comrades—perhaps I will be DEPORTED before these vibrant pages will be read by the Italian workers who suffer, aspire, struggle. Oh! that torch will no longer shine the light it did![47]

Luigi Galleani, the dominant figure among the Italian-born anarchists, had already been deported. When news of the death of his comrade Andrea Salsedo, who either jumped or was pushed from a Park Row building while in the custody of the Department of Justice, reached Galleani, he responded with this grotesque caricature of the Statue of Liberty: "This monstrous collossus [*sic*], this republic of the heart of anthracite, with the forehead of ice, with the goiterous throat; this statue of cretinism . . . whose hands are armed with a whip, from whose lips are suspended a knife and a revolver . . ."[48] In the eyes of Galleani, the Mother of Exiles had been transmogrified into a murderous monster.

In the aftermath of World War I, increasingly stringent immigration legislation left the Golden Door only slightly ajar. The nativists won a complete victory with the National Origins Act of 1924, which was based on blatantly racist principles. Oblivious to the irony, President Calvin Coolidge designated the statue a national monument in that same year. A French wit quipped: "We, too, raise monuments to the illustrious dead."[49] Curiously, the statue was not used very much to oppose these restrictionist policies, perhaps because English-language publications and their cartoonists, for the most part, supported the policies. One exception, the Yiddish *Groyser Kundes* (The Big Stick), employed the statue in cartoons opposing immigration restriction: a senator is portrayed reading the proposed quota law by the light of the torch of the statue, and President Warren G. Harding is depicted in the act of snuffing out Liberty's torch by his endorsement of the quota bill.[50]

The Statue of Liberty was little invoked in the ideological debates of the 1920s, a decade of decreasing immigration and rampant bigotry. Economic depression brought immigration to its lowest point in the 1930s; in fact, the United States suffered a net out-migration for the first time in its history. Significantly, the statue was not featured in New Deal iconography. Although a gala celebration was held in honor of Miss Liberty's Golden Jubilee in 1936, a somber note was sounded by various speakers who called attention to the threat posed by the rise of totalitarian regimes. Speaking from the base of the statue, President Franklin D. Roosevelt voiced the theme of the New World as "mankind's second chance." At a time of intensifying xenophobia, he chose to emphasize the positive contributions of immigrants. "By their effort and devotion," he affirmed, "they made the New World's freedom safer, richer, more far-reaching, more capable of growth." But the president consigned the role of immigration to the past, as he concluded, "[W]e have within our shores today the materials out of which we shall continue to build an ever better home for liberty."[51] Other speakers endorsed the view that the statue no longer served as a magnet to draw freedom-seekers from the Old World; rather, it had become "a symbol of the noble traditions and ideals of America."[52]

Such a self-congratulatory mood was not universally shared. In an article ironically titled "Mother of Exiles," James Benét cited the deportation by the United States of refugees from Nazi Germany and Fascist Italy as a counterpoint to FDR's speech. In a "Happy Birthday" to the Statue of Liberty editorial, the Communist *Daily Worker* observed that more people left than entered the United States in 1935, eight thousand of them deportees, and chided the president for declaring "liberty" a living thing while the constitutional rights of immigrants were being violated.[53] In fact, during the thirties, the Mother of Exiles looked the other way as Jews and others fleeing persecution futilely sought asylum in the United States. In a cartoon titled "Is My Face Red!" Liberty shamefacedly casts her eyes down as displaced persons are barred from entry.[54] With the outbreak of war in 1939, fears of "un-American" activities culminated in legislation that not only barred "subversives" from naturalization but also deported aliens who had been members of the Communist party at any time. Hugo Gellert, Hungarian-born artist and *New Masses* contributor, drew a sketch of the foreign-born in stocks with a dejected Liberty in the background to protest the Alien Registration Act of 1940, which required that aliens be registered and fingerprinted.[55]

Challenging powerful nativist currents in the thirties, socialist and populist movements celebrated the lives of common people in all their ethnic and regional diversity. Immigrants, workers, farmers were apotheosized as quintessential Americans, and the Statue of Liberty was reclaimed as the symbol of cultural democracy.[56] Louis Adamic, a writer and immigrant from Slovenia who was the leading prophet of an America in which all racial and ethnic elements would be prized and harmonized, proposed "an intellectual-emotional synthesis of the old and new America; of the Mayflower and the steerage . . . of the Liberty Bell and the Statue of Liberty." More than any other person, he revitalized the idea of the statue as the Mother of Immigrants.[57]

In a cartoon of 1940, Liberty bows to embrace her children—"Americans All!"—but they are without exception of European extraction.[58] Race remained the major stumbling block in the path of the movement for cultural democracy of the thirties and forties. The statue was not featured in World War II propaganda as it had been during World War I. Was this because "race" had replaced "nationality" as the major challenge to American unity? For American Indians, African Americans, Hispanic Americans, and Asian Americans, the statue, for obvious reasons, lacked the mythic power that it held for European Americans.[59]

For several decades after World War II, American immigration policy remained restrictionist and discriminatory. Despite the uprooting of millions by the war and changes in national boundaries, the United States only slowly and grudgingly responded to the plight of the so-called displaced persons. Herb Block in a 1947 cartoon portrayed a snobbish Liberty looking haughtily through a lorgnette and holding up her hand in an act of rejection, while Harry Truman and Thomas Dewey ask, "What happened to the one we used to have?"[60]

The Cold War and the resulting anti-Communist hysteria stimulated a resurgent nativism directed at alleged subversives. This McCarthyism, as it came to be called, resulted in the Internal Security Act of 1950 and the Immigration and Nationality Act of 1952, which gave administrative officials broad discretionary powers over exclusion, deportation, and even denaturalization. A cartoon by Daniel R. Fitzpatrick in 1952 pictures the Lady with the Torch bowed under the weight of chain and balls bearing the names of Louis Ragni and Carl Latva, both threatened with deportation because of past membership in the Communist party.[61]

Although they championed such illiberal measures, politicians still paid lip service to the ideal of liberty. Representative Francis Walters, a leading advocate of immigration restriction, introduced a resolution in 1952 designating October 28 as Statue of Liberty Day in recognition of this "welcoming beacon to the oppressed and persecuted of all lands and faiths." Also, in 1954 the U.S. Post Office issued a series of stamps featuring Bartholdi and the Statue of Liberty. In 1956 Congress approved a plan to develop a museum of immigration at the base of the statue and changed the name from Bedloe's Island to Liberty Island.[62] Now that the influx of Lazarus's "huddled masses" appeared to be a thing of the past, it was safe to enshrine them in a historical temple.

But the politicans had miscalculated; the next chapter in the saga of American immigration was about to begin. Vigorous lobbying resulted in the enactment of liberalized immigration legislation in 1965, which scrapped the racial quota system and opened the country to persons from all parts of the world. President John F. Kennedy had strongly supported this measure, but it was Lyndon Baines Johnson who signed it into law at the base of the Statue of Liberty on October 3, 1965. On that occasion he declared: "Now, under this monument which has welcomed so many to our shores, the American nation returns to the finest of its traditions today. . . . And today we can all believe that the lamp of this grand old lady is brighter and the golden door that she guards gleams more brilliantly."[63] Cartoonists had a field day depicting LBJ as a lamplighter and as a referee holding up the arm of the statue who has just knocked out the "quota system."[64]

On signing the 1965 immigration law, President Johnson observed that the legislation probably would not have much practical effect. Its consequences, however, have been dramatic and far-reaching. By the late seventies, the annual number of immigrants began to approach a million, a volume unseen since the early twenties. Moreover, the primary origins of the new arrivals were no longer Europe and Canada, but Asia and Latin America. Immigration policy was once again hotly debated. The rallying cry of the restrictionists was, "We have lost control of our borders." A 1980 cartoon by Clifford Baldowski of the *Atlanta Constitution* shows a perplexed statue awash in a sea of humanity, with the statue shouting "Help!" Cartoons like this one expressed a fear of liberalized immigration that the Cuban-based Mariel boatlift at the time raised to the level of panic.[65]

The report of the Select Commission on Immigration and Refugee Policy, issued in 1981, was, on the whole, liberal in its recommendations. The Reagan administration, however, took a hardnosed, conservative position. "Reagan's Immigration Plan," the title of a 1981 Bob Englehart cartoon depicting the president as the statue armed with a shotgun, shows a mean public spirit.[66] The United States Coast Guard interdicted boats carrying refugees from Haiti on the high seas, and the Immigration and Naturalization Service conducted sweeps of factories and fields for illegal aliens. In a cartoon by Signe Wilkinson, titled "O.K. You Huddled Masses, I Know You're in Here," the statue is depicted as an INS agent searching a sweatshop.[67] Cartoonists such as John Trever and Doug Marlette revised Emma Lazarus's sonnet to reflect a rising sentiment of hostility toward immigrants from non-European countries (fig. 4.10).[68]

By one of those curious twists of history, Congress and the administration were debating the terms of tougher immigration legislation exactly at the time when the Statue of Liberty–Ellis Island Commission was planning centennial observances and undertaking major repairs to the statue. With the refurbishing of the statue in progress, cartoonist Don Wright in 1983 suggested a different kind of statue renovation. In his cartoon the statue has discarded its torch and in its place shows a thumbs-down pose.[69]

It was a coincidence that the Immigration Reform and Control Act was passed in 1986, the centennial year of the statue. The law addressed the problem of undocumented immigration by providing penalties for employers hiring illegal aliens on the one hand and by offering legalization under certain terms to undocumented immigrants on the other. A Clyde Wells cartoon titled "My Melting Pot Runneth Over" shows Liberty holding on to a pot teeming with immigrants, her torch pointing downward, as if it were broken.[70]

Although the jet plane has replaced the steamship as the main means of transportation to the United States, and Los Angeles has replaced New York as the major port of entry, the Statue of Liberty

Fig. 4.10. Statue of Liberty as "Mother of Exiles." United States immigration policy in recent years has been widely perceived as favoring refugees from Communist countries and persons with exceptional talents, while discriminating against poor people who may be fleeing repressive regimes such as Haiti's. This 1982 cartoon, by Doug Marlette, offers a critical perspective. Reprinted by permission of Doug Marlette and Creators Syndicate.

retains its power to evoke the immigrant myth so central to the American identity. Today's immigrants, arriving in airports, landing on isolated beaches, or crossing the borders, are not greeted by the Mother of Exiles. They do not have its blessing, nor do they feel a special attachment to it. And yet the power of the idea of liberty still radiates from that freshly gilded torch. In recent years the statue has been more often called upon to oppose restrictionist policies and to defend the rights of immigrants than ever before in its long career. Recently it was evoked in a protest against the forced repatriation of Haitian boat people.[71]

The Statue of Liberty, however, is a fickle goddess; it has served various causes and masters. No oracle, it speaks to us only with "silent lips" unless we put the words in its mouth, as did Emma Lazarus. As are all monuments, it is a hollow vessel waiting to be filled with whatever meaning we choose to pour into it.[72] What will be the role of the colossus in the future: Mother of Exiles or Guardian of the Gates? Only time—and the American people—will tell.

NOTES

This essay was first presented at the symposium "Liberty: As Idea, Icon, and Engineering Feat," held on October 19, 1985. In its present form, the essay is much revised and expanded. For assistance in identifying and locating images and texts relating to the Statue of Liberty, I wish to acknowledge the generous help of John Appel, Paul Avrich, Stephan F. Brumberg, Frank Costigliola, Roger Daniels, Alan Dawley, Gianfausto Rosoli, Phyllis Montgomery, and Linda Watson.

1. The Statue of Liberty has been the subject of scores of volumes and hundreds of articles. Among these, I have found the following particularly helpful in the preparation of this essay: Marvin Trachtenberg, *The Statue of Liberty* (New York: Viking, 1976); André Gschaedler, *True Light on the Statue of Liberty and Its Creator* (Narbeth, Pa.: Livingston Publishing, 1966); Hertha Pauli and E. B. Ashton, *I Lift My Lamp: The Way of a Symbol* (New York and London: Appleton-Century-Crofts, 1948; and Rodman Gilder, *The Statue of Liberty Enlightening the World* (New York: New York Trust Company, 1943). The centennial inspired a surge of publications. Particularly handsome and informative are Christian Blanchet and Bertrand Dard, *Statue de la Liberté: Le livre du centenaire* (Paris: Edition Comet's, 1984); and Leslie Allen, *Liberty: The Statue and the American Dream* (New York: Statue of Liberty–Ellis Island Foundation, 1985). On the global dissemination of reproductions of the statue itself, see Edward L. Kallop, Jr., comp., *Images of Liberty: Models and Reductions of the Statue of Liberty 1867–1917. Special Centennial Exhibition January 25–February 15, 1986* (New York: Christie, Manson, and Woods International, 1985).

2. On the changing meanings ascribed to the statue by Americans, see, in addition to titles cited above: George M. Dembo, "The Statue of Liberty in Posters: Creation of an American Icon," *P.S.: Quarterly Journal of the Poster Society* 1 (Winter 1985–86): 18–21; Roger A. Fischer, "Oddity, Icon, Challenge: The Statue of Liberty in American Cartoon Art, 1879–1986," *Journal of American Culture* 9 (Winter 1986): 63–81; Oscar Handlin, *Statue of Liberty* (New York: Newsweek Books, 1971); John Higham, "The Transformation of the Statue of Liberty," in *Send These to Me: Immigrants in Urban America*, rev. ed. (Baltimore: Johns Hopkins University Press, 1984), 71–80; John J. Appel and Selma Appel, "The Huddled Masses and the Little Red Schoolhouse," in *American Education and the European Immigrant:*

1840–1940, ed. Bernard J. Weiss (Urbana: University of Illinois Press, 1982), 18–30. *Taking Liberty with the Lady, by Cartoonists around the World*, comp. and ed. Dani Aguila (Nashville: Eagle Nest Publishing, 1986), is a useful collection of cartoons. Since this essay was written, another relevant article by John Higham has appeared: "America in Person: The Evolution of Relevant Symbols," *Amerikanstudien. American Studies* 36 (1991): 473–84.

3. Quoted in Allen, *Liberty*, 9; but for critical views of the operations of the Statue of Liberty–Ellis Island Foundation and Commission, see Lynn Johnson, "Ellis Island: Historic Preservation from the Supply Side," *Radical History Review*, nos. 28–30 (September 1984): 57–68; Roberta Brandes Gratz and Eric Fettmann, "Iacocca's Golden Door: The Selling of Miss Liberty," *Nation* 241 (November 9, 1985): 465–66. For a comprehensive history of the renovation project, see H. Ross Holland, *Idealists, Scoundrels, and the Lady: The Memoirs of an Insider in the Statue of Liberty–Ellis Island Project* (Urbana and Chicago: University of Illinois Press, 1993).

4. On the genesis and meaning of the statue, see Blanchet and Dard, *Statue de la Liberté*, 14–46; for a feminist interpretation, see Marina Warner, *Monuments and Maidens: The Allegory of the Female Form* (New York: Atheneum, 1985), 1–15. On the French background, Tristam B. Johnson, *Liberty Enlightening the World* (New York: N.p., 1986), is useful.

5. I find a wider circulation and appreciation of Lazarus's poem than have Oscar Handlin and John Higham. "The New Colossus" was printed in *The Poems of Emma Lazarus* (Boston and New York: Houghton Mifflin, 1888), 1:202–3, and Ross Conway Stone, *A Way to See and Study the Statue of Liberty Enlightening the World* (New York: Bullion Publishing, 1887), 7. Stone also made this point: "As the navies of the world, guided by its light, pass by the mighty flambeau to our docks, the dullest tar or lowliest immigrant is plainly told in the universal language of symbolism that he is in the land of liberty" (5). James Russell Lowell, poet laureate, wrote to Lazarus: "I must write again to say how much I like your sonnet about the statue—much better than I like the statue itself. But your sonnet gives its subject a raison d'être which it wanted before quite as much as it wants a pedestal" (quoted in Doris Brown, "Lazarus and the Promised Land(s)," *Moment* [May 1985]: 49–52).

6. Quoted in Gschaedler, *True Light on the Statue of Liberty*, 135. The following two quotes are also from ibid., 43, 116–17.

7. Quoted in Pauli and Ashton, *I Lift My Lamp*, 321.

8. As Marina Warner observes, the Statue of Liberty soon took on the character of a mother: "We are all her children, she speaks to us in the voice of

a mother. . . . Emma Lazarus's famous flight of rhetoric dissolves the harshness of Liberty's countenance, and she becomes a mother of mercy" (*Monuments and Maidens*, 11). Although the stern visage of the statue was modeled after Bartholdi's mother, he would not have been pleased by the interpretation of his Liberté as the Mother of the Immigrants. The imperious sculptor angrily denounced the "monstrous plan" to build an immigration station at Bedloe's Island as a "desecration" (Ann Novotny, *Strangers at the Door: Ellis Island, Castle Garden, and the Great Migration to America*, abridged ed. [Toronto, New York, London: Bantam Pathfinder Editions, 1974], 96).

9. *New York Sunday News Magazine*, February 19, 1984, 49.

10. Edward Corsi, *In the Shadow of Liberty* (New York: Macmillan, 1935), 3–4.

11. Edward A. Steiner, *On the Trail of the Immigrant* (New York: F. H. Revell, 1906), 60. Similar testimonies abound in immigrant memoirs; see the excerpts in Harlan D. Unrau, *Ellis Island Statue of Liberty*, New York–New Jersey Historic Resource Study, 3 vols. (Denver: U.S. Department of the Interior, National Park Service, 1984), 3:1083–113; for a particularly affecting collection, see Lynne Bundesen, ed., *Dear Miss Liberty: Letters to the Statue of Liberty* (Salt Lake City: Peregrine Smith Books, 1986); also see the oral histories in David M. Brownstone, Irene M. Franck, and Douglass L. Brownstone, *Island of Hope, Island of Tears* (New York: Penguin Books, 1986).

12. Carla Bianco, *The Two Rosetos* (Bloomington and London: Indiana University Press, 1974), 89. Another example of the syncretism of traditional religious symbols with the statue is the menorah fashioned out of miniature Statues of Liberty created by Manfred Anson, an immigrant from Germany (cover of the Hebrew Union College–JIR 1991–1992 calendar). I thank Stephan F. Brumberg for providing me with this item.

13. Hungarian Postal Workers to President Herbert Hoover, March 4, 1932, Record Group 59, Document #763, 72119/12523, Diplomatic Branch, National Archives. Frank Costigliola, who used this illustration for the cover of his book, *Awkward Dominion: American Political, Economic, and Cultural Relations with Europe, 1919–1933* (Ithaca, N.Y.: Cornell University Press, 1984), provided me with the document location.

14. "Welcome to the Land of Freedom," *Frank Leslie's Weekly*, July 2, 1887.

15. *The Graphic* (London) 45 (February 13, 1892): 204. Illustrating the wide dissemination of such images, a similar composition was used for the cover of the book *Za Okeanom* (Across the Ocean) (L'vi: Nakaladom T-va "Ridna Shkola," 1930) by Lev Iasinchuk.

16. An example of a steamship line guidebook that carries on its cover the familiar scene of immigrants viewing the Statue of Liberty is *Dall'Italia a New York: Guida dell'emigrante 1902* of the Navigazione Generale Italiana. I am indebted to Gianfausto Rosoli for this illustration. Postcards issued by Cunard, Holland-America, and other shipping lines also feature the statue with their steamships.

17. Yivo Institute for Jewish Research, *A Guide to Yivo's Landsmanshaften Archive* (New York: Yivo Institute for Jewish Research, 1986), reproduces several title pages of benevolent society constitutions featuring the Statue of Liberty. Other examples of the statue in ethnic iconography include the cover of *Americky'Sbornik*, a New York Czech publication of 1898, the masthead of *Svoboda*, a Ukrainian newspaper, from 1921 forward, the covers of *Armenian Encyclopedic Almanac 1925* (Boston, 1924) and *Tpetr Khnxeyka* (Ukrainian third reader) (L'viv, 1931).

18. Examples of this genre of publications sporting the statue on the cover or title page include Mary F. Severance, *A Guide to American Citizenship* (N.p., 1909); Sara R. O'Brien, *English for Foreigners* (New York: Houghton Mifflin, 1909); Edwin Noah Hardy, *A Manual for American Citizenship* (New York: American Tract Society, 1919); Thomas Burgess, *Foreign-Born Americans and Their Children* (New York: Department of Missions and Church Extension of the Episcopal Church, 1921?); William E. Scott, *Citizenship for New Americans* (Saint Paul, Minn.: Scott-Mitchell Publishing Company, 1923; 2d ed., 1925); Dwight C. Morgan, *The Foreign Born in the United States* (New York: American Committee for Protection of Foreign Born, 1936); Francis Kalnay, comp. and ed., *The New American: A Handbook of Necessary Information for Aliens, Refugees, and New Citizens* (New York: Greenberg, 1941).

19. "Statue of Liberty Pageant," P.S. 188, Manhattan, c. 1910. This photograph was provided by Stephan F. Brumberg.

20. On nativism and immigration policy, see John Higham, *Strangers in the Land: Patterns of American Nativism 1860–1925* (New York: Atheneum, 1975); Barbara Solomon, *Ancestors and Immigrants: A Changing New England Tradition* (Cambridge, Mass.: Harvard University Press, 1956); Stuart C. Miller, *The Unwelcome Immigrant: The American Image of the Chinese* (Berkeley: University of California Press, 1969).

21. *American Missionary* 39 (October 1885). I am indebted to Roger Daniels for this reference.

22. Higham, *Strangers in the Land*, 54–55; for a full account of the event and its consequences, see Paul Avrich, *The Haymarket Tragedy* (Princeton, N.J.: Princeton University Press, 1984).

23. *Orations and Speeches of Chauncey M. Depew*, ed. John Denison Champlin (New York: Privately printed, 1910), vol. 1, *Orations and Memorial Addresses*, 107. Emphasis added. See also Pauli and Ashton, *I Lift My Lamp*, 322.

24. On immigration and naturalization policies with regard to radicals and their constitutional ramifications, see Rudolph J. Vecoli, "Immigration, Naturalization, and the Constitution," *Studi emigrazione (Rome)* 24 (March 1987): 75–100.

25. *America* 2 (Chicago), May 30, 1889, cover.

26. Emma Goldman, *Living My Life* (New York: Alfred A. Knopf, 1934), 11, 717.

27. "The Future Emigrant Lodging House," *Judge* 18 (April 12, 1890): 16. Fresh arrivals ascend a ladder on the way to the "International Tenement House," stopping along the way for spaghetti at Carlo Italiano's or lager beer at Fritz Gurlick's. At the very top of the statue is the red flag of the anarchist headquarters.

28. *Judge* 18 (March 22, 1890).

29. *New York Evening Telegram*, September 10, 1892.

30. Thomas Bailey Aldrich, *Unguarded Gates and Other Poems* (Boston and New York: Houghton, Mifflin, 1895), 15–17. On Aldrich, see Charles E. Samuels, *Thomas Bailey Aldrich* (New York: Twayne Publishers, 1965).

31. This and other postcards cited are from the author's personal collection.

32. O. Henry, *Sixes and Sevens* (Garden City, N.Y.: Doubleday, Page, 1916), 214–19.

33. Richard H. Schneider photographed this immigrant family, standing on Ellis Island as they awaited processing.

34. *The Autobiography of Emanuel Carnevali* (New York: Horizon Press, c. 1967), 197–201.

35. Aleksandra Kollontai, "The Statue of Liberty: The End of 1916," in *Selected Articles and Speeches*, comp. I. M. Dazhina et al., trans. Cynthia Carlile (New York: International Publishers, 1984), 112–15.

36. *New York Times*, December 3, 1916; Pauli and Ashton, *I Lift My Lamp*, 304, 317–18.

37. "Signal by President Bathes Liberty Statue in Flood of Light," *New York Times*, December 3, 1916.

38. *Ai Compagni, ai simpatizzanti e agli amici della "Questione sociale,"* March 28, 1908. Manifesto in Nettlau Archive, International Institute of Social

History, Amsterdam. The translations from this and other Italian texts are the author's. For a further development of this theme, see Rudolph J. Vecoli, "'Free Country': The American Republic Viewed by the Italian Left, 1880–1920," in *In the Shadow of the Statue of Liberty: Immigrants, Workers, and Citizens in the American Republic*, ed. Marianne Debouzy (Saint-Denis, France: Presses Universitaires de Vincennes, 1988), 35–56.

39. *Free Country!* (N.p., 1908?).

40. *L'Internazionale* (Philadelphia) 1 (January 15, 1909): 30.

41. The quote is from the report of Agent 40S in *U.S. Military Intelligence Reports: Surveillance of Radicals in the United States, 1917–1941*, microfilm ed. (University Publications of America), reel 1, document 10110–56.

42. Louis Giclas, *The Conscript of 1917. Bartholdi How to View the Beacon Landmark*, rev. ed. (New York, 1938), 6, 14. According to Giclas, the Statue of Liberty was used as the central motif in twenty-three of thirty posters for the Liberty Bond campaign. See also Shaun Aubitz and Gail F. Stern, "Ethnic Images in World War I Posters," *Journal of American Culture* 9 (Winter 1986): 83–89. According to Aubitz and Stern, it was not until World War I that "the image of Lady Liberty began to be widely recognized as a national symbol" (Dembo, "Statue of Liberty in Posters," 19).

43. "Remember Your First Thrill of American Liberty" is the title of one of the most famous patriotic posters of World War I; it was used by the U.S. government to encourage the purchase of war bonds to finance the war effort.

44. Frederick C. Luebke, *Bonds of Loyalty: German-Americans and World War I* (DeKalb, Ill.: Northern Illinois University Press, 1974); William Preston, *Aliens and Dissenters: Federal Suppression of Radicals, 1903–1933* (Cambridge, Mass.: Harvard University Press, 1963); Robert K. Murray, *Red Scare: A Study in National Hysteria, 1919–1920* (Minneapolis: University of Minnesota Press, 1955).

45. Allen, *Liberty the Statue*, 248.

46. *The Liberator* 3 (February 1920): 4. "The Sailing of the Buford," by Boardman Robinson.

47. *Guardia Rossa* (New York), c. May 1920, 1.

48. "Tutto l'obbrobio!" *Cronaca sovversiva* (Turin), June 12, 1920.

49. Quoted in Pauli and Ashton, *I Lift My Lamp*, 315; Handlin, *Statue of Liberty*, 64.

50. *Groyser Kundes* (New York), January 7, 1921, and July 13, 1923. A Zionist socialist publication, *Groyser Kundes* frequently incorporated the Statue of Liberty in its cartoons. I am grateful to John J. Appel for copies of these illustrations. A study of ethnic publications may reveal a more extensive use of the statue as symbol than was true of the English-language press.

51. *New York Times*, October 29, 1936. An editorial applauded the president's emphasis on the unity and cultural homogeneity of the American people despite their diverse origins. The text of the speech is in *Nothing to Fear: The Selected Addresses of Franklin Delano Roosevelt 1932–1945*, ed. B. D. Zevin (Boston: Houghton Mifflin, 1946), 69–72.

52. *Scholastic* 27 (November 2, 1935): 16; *School Life* 22 (October 1936): 35–36; *National Education Association Journal* 24 (November 1935): 245.

53. James Benét, "Mother of Exiles," *New Republic* 89 (November 25, 1936): 108–9; *New York Daily Worker*, October 28, 1936. Employing popular front rhetoric, the *Daily Worker* editorial read in part: "For fifty years you've stood there holding up the torch of liberty to the oppressed of all lands. For fifty years you've been the symbol of what this country meant to Jefferson and Jackson and Lincoln, of the dream that they had. A symbol or a shadow? Reality or illusion? Terre Haute, Tampa, El Centro—is this the dream of the Founding Fathers? This savage trampling on the Bill of Rights, this rule of fascist violence and terror?"

54. Ned White, "Is My Face Red!" July 14, 1941; reprinted in Aguila, *Taking Liberty with the Lady*, 45.

55. Vito Marcantonio, *The Registration of Aliens* (New York: American Committee for the Protection of the Foreign Born, 1940); Mary Ryan Gallery, *Hugo Gellert* (New York: Mary Ryan Gallery, 1986). Gellert repeatedly used the figure of a downcast Statue of Liberty as a biting commentary on American society.

56. Richard Weiss, "Ethnicity and Reform: Minorities and Ambience of the Depression Years," *Journal of American History* 66 (December 1979): 269–94; Nicholas Montalto, *A History of the Intercultural Educational Movement 1924–1941* (New York: Garland, 1982); Aleksander Posern-Zielinski, "Americanization Programmes for Immigrants and Ethnic Cultures in the United States during the Inter-War Years," *Ethnologia Polonia* 9 (1983): 149–82.

57. Among Louis Adamic's many writings, the most relevant is his essay "Plymouth Rock and Ellis Island," in *From Many Lands* (New York: Harper and Brothers, 1940), 291–301; on Adamic, see Henry A. Christian, *Louis Adamic: A Checklist* (Kent, O.: Kent State University Press, 1971); Robert F.

Harney, "E Pluribus Unum: Louis Adamic and the Meaning of Ethnic History," *Journal of Ethnic Studies* 14 (Spring 1986): 29–46; Rudolph J. Vecoli, "Louis Adamic and the Contemporary Search for Roots," *Ethnic Studies* (Australia) 2 (1978): 29–35; *Louis Adamic Symposium*, ed. Janez Stanonik (Ljubljana, Slovenia: Univerza Edvarda Kardelja v Ljubljani, 1981); Higham, "Transformation of the Statue of Liberty," 77–78.

58. "Americans All!" *Detroit Free Press*, June 19, 1941, by cartoonist Arthur Poinier; reprinted in Aguila, *Taking Liberty with the Lady*, 10. The "Americans All—Immigrants All" slogan was also employed by the U.S. Office of Education in 1939 as the title of a radio series devoted to the "contribution of various cultural groups to the economic, social and political development of the United States." A brochure promoting the series bore that title and featured on its cover the Statue of Liberty reviewing the panorama of American history, from Pilgrims through immigrants and pioneers (including blacks sitting on cotton bales on a levee!) to contemporary farmers and workers. For an insightful commentary on this source, see Esther Romeyn, "Join the World Cruise: An Excursion into America's Mythical International Village" (unpublished paper, 1991).

59. Attitudes of non-European Americans remain to be studied, but the following is suggestive of an ambivalent, if not hostile, view of the statue's symbolism. Studs Terkel reports the experience of a black GI returning from Europe: "The white soldiers up on deck said, 'There she is!' They're talking about the Statue of Liberty. There's a great outburst. I'm down below and I'm sayin', Hell, I'm not goin' up there. Damn that. All of a sudden, I found myself with tears, cryin' and saying the same thing they were saying" (*"The Good War": An Oral History of World War Two* [New York: Pantheon, 1984], 282). In 1965, the Black Liberation Front unsuccessfully planned to blow up the statue, intending to render the "damned old bitch" headless and torchless (Barbara Blumberg, *Celebrating the Immigrant: An Administrative History of the Statue of Liberty's National Monument 1952–1982*, Cultural Resource Management Study, no. 10 [National Park Service, U.S. Department of the Interior, 1985], 13). Note also James Baldwin's bitter comments in the documentary film *The Statue of Liberty*, by Kenneth L. Burns, and the statement by then Atlanta mayor Andrew Young: "No one in the black community is really excited about the Statue of Liberty. We came here on slave ships, not via Ellis Island" (*USA Today*, July 3, 1986, quoted in Robert Asher and Charles Stephenson, eds., *Labor Divided: Race and Ethnicity in United States Labor Struggles 1835–1960* [Albany: State University Press of New York, 1990], 3).

60. *Common Ground* 7 (Winter 1947): 85; reprinted from the *Washington Post*.

61. Daniel R. Fitzpatrick, *St. Louis Post-Dispatch*, August 26, 1952.

62. Blumberg, *Celebrating the Immigrant*, 10–11.

63. *Congressional Quarterly* 23 (October 1965): 2063–64. A proclamation issued by Johnson in 1965 adding Ellis Island to the Statue of Liberty National Monument declared: "[T]he Statue of Liberty is a symbol to the world of the dreams and aspirations which have drawn so many millions of immigrants to America" (quoted in August Bolino, *The Ellis Island Source Book* [Washington, D.C.: Kensington Historical Press, 1985], 54–55).

64. "LBJ's Proposed Immigration Changes," *Washington Daily News*, January 14, 1965; "And Still Champion," *Albany (N.Y.) Times-Union*, January 15, 1965.

65. "The Statue of Liberty in a Sea of Humanity," *Commercial Appeal*, n.d., by Bill Garner; "Help!" *Atlanta Constitution*, May 9, 1980, by Clifford Baldowski; reprinted in Aguila, *Taking Liberty with the Lady*, 35, 43.

66. "Reagan's Immigration Plan," *Hartford Courant*, 1981, by Bob Englehart; reprinted in Aguila, *Taking Liberty with the Lady*, 134.

67. "O.K. You Huddled Masses, I Know You're in Here," *San Jose Mercury News*, n.d., cartoonist Signe Wilkinson; reprinted in Aguila, *Taking Liberty with the Lady*, 104.

68. "Give Me 50,000, Etc.," *Albuquerque Journal*, 1981, by cartoonist John Trever; "Give Me Your Rich, Etc.," *Charlotte Observer*, 1982, by cartoonist Doug Marlette; reprinted in *The Gang of Eight*, intro. Tom Brokaw.

69. "As Long As It Had to Be Repaired, They Thought It Should Accurately Reflect Immigration Policy," *Miami News*, 1983, by cartoonist Don Wright; reprinted in *The Gang of Eight*.

70. "My Melting Pot Runneth Over," *Augusta Chronicle*, 1984, by cartoonist Clyde Wells.

71. *Minneapolis Star and Tribune*, December 7, 1991; reprinted from *Palm Beach Post*. Viewing the Statue of Liberty, the son asks his father: "What is the torch for?" The father answers: "To burn Haitian boats."

72. As Marina Warner put it: "The statue's hollowness, which we occupy literally when we make the ascent to Liberty's equally empty head, is a prerequisite for symbols with infinite powers of endurance and adaptability. She is given meaning by us, and it can change, according to what we see or want" (*Monuments and Maidens*, 11).

Liberty as Image and Icon

BERTRAND DARD

he Statue of Liberty has never aged. Rather, Liberty has successfully adapted herself to a multitude of causes and campaigns, to the many diverse expectations and goals with which she has been identified at various times in her history.

Cartoonists and writers have employed her image to support the liberalization of immigration laws, attack the inadequacies of government, condemn war, mobilize sympathy for the poor, and advocate or condemn countless other causes. Business firms and manufacturers have used Liberty's image to market pears grown in California, introduce a new line of Parisian perfumes, advertise liquors, sell cheeses, and promote many other kinds of products (fig. 5.1). Liberty has graced the postage stamps of numerous countries of the world, even some ruled by dictatorships.

Yet the core symbolism of Liberty survives intact. Catalyst for the preoccupations and the woes of humankind, Liberty has served at one time or another as confessor, oracle, and keeper of the collective conscience of American society (and, indeed, of other societies overseas). Liberty is the premier monumental icon of modern times.

Fig. 5.1. "Liberty Enlightening the World as to the Best Six-Cord Thread in the Market." Businesses used mass advertising and the image of Liberty to bolster the appeal of their products. In this advertising card (c. 1885), the Merrick Thread Company touts its cotton sewing thread. The statue's likeness was used in advertisements even before the monument itself was opened in October 1886. Reprinted from the Warshaw Collection, by permission of the Archives Center, National Museum of American History, Smithsonian Institution, Washington, D.C.

If Liberty had been simply a work that a group of men created a century ago, and her significance had been limited to that fact, she would be just another tourist attraction—a monument to a time past, a relic of bygone years. Yet Liberty's symbolic force, and the devotion that is lavished on her by her admirers, simply grow stronger with the passage of time. What accounts for the power of her image and her message?

Two aspects of the Statue of Liberty—one external, a set of circumstances; the other internal, a set of intrinsic qualities—can provide an explanation for her symbolic impact. The first involves the events of the late nineteenth and the twentieth centuries, each of which has added rich new dimensions to her meaning. The second reflects the depth of Liberty's visual representation and imagery.

The impressive development of the United States in the latter part of the nineteenth century and the first half of the twentieth century made a strong impression in countries throughout the world. America's incredible economic expansion, the dynamism and drive of its complex society, and the prosperity and progress that seemed to characterize the nation at that time fascinated people everywhere.

Yet the enormous economic growth was not achieved without cost. Social and economic conflicts multiplied, as did wealth. Vast industrial complexes and corporations emerged, and so, too, did problems of labor management and labor strife. Industrial strikes and political struggles between workers and the owners of industry developed in many places. In the early years of Liberty's installation in New York Harbor, she came to symbolize the dynamism and prosperity of America's free society. As industrial conflict escalated, however, the statue took on the opposite meaning in some quarters. Critics debunked Liberty as irrelevant to the aspirations of workers and to the ongoing struggle over economic justice. A 1912 illustration in the British periodical *Puck* captured this disillusionment by showing Liberty dethroned by King Dollar, who was represented by a golden calf.

When World War I began, Liberty acquired yet another set of meanings. At the initiative of Herbert Hoover, then director of a federal agency known as the American Relief Administration (and later president of the country), the Statue of Liberty was enlisted alongside the images of Uncle Sam and Columbia in advertisements for the sale of war bonds. The statue became a mascot for those endeavoring to rally citizens to the war effort (fig. 5.2).

Liberty as a symbol of American patriotism was revived in 1940, during World War II. The Allied victory was, above all, a victory of democracy over dictatorship and totalitarianism. So the symbolism of the statue was reshaped to depict the march of progress among democratic governments throughout the world. The spread of democracy has repeatedly been linked to the Statue of Liberty.

A dramatic example of Liberty's recurring democratic symbolism arose in June 1989 in Beijing, China—not in a society that had adopted democracy but rather among a people who had embraced, against great odds, the aspiration of living in a free society. The student-led movement for democracy in Beijing's Tiananmen Square was marked by the construction from Styrofoam plastic and plaster of a replica of the Statue of Liberty that came to be known as the Goddess of Democracy. One such statue was erected near the site of the student uprising; others were placed at the United Nations in

Fig. 5.2. "You Buy a Liberty Bond Lest I Perish." C. R. Macauley's poster was used in the government's first Liberty Loan campaign in 1917, encouraging citizens to help pay for American participation in World War I. It was during this period that the image of Liberty was first linked to pro-war and patriotic feelings, appearing on advertisements and billboards everywhere—and nearly displacing the other popular image used for such purposes, that of Uncle Sam. Reprinted by permission of National Park Service, Statue of Liberty National Monument.

New York, in front of the Chinese embassy in Washington, D.C., and in Europe. Each of these Chinese renderings of Liberty served as a rallying point for democratic reform. The Chinese Goddess of Democracy demonstrated once again the evolving symbolism of Liberty—not simply as an embodiment of personal freedom but as the representation of the spirit of a free society and of self-government.

Yet despite the Statue of Liberty's great popularity during many of the last hundred years, in the two decades immediately following the unveiling in New York Harbor in October 1886, popular interest in the statue declined. The events of that era before World War I—the technological and economic breakthroughs, in particular—diverted public attention from the statue and its democratic symbolism. One new area of interest proved to be the transportation advances of flying machines and automobiles. Another was urban growth and the building of skyscrapers. America's westward movement also gained prominence in the popular imagination. This trend of growing indifference to Liberty, however, was soon to be halted in a decisive way.

Liberty was poised for a remarkable transformation, owing to the statue's location on Bedloe's Island in New York Harbor. The great drama of European immigration, which had been gathering momentum during the latter half of the nineteenth century, once again thrust the Statue of Liberty into the center of national and international attention. Of all the external conditions that have impinged upon Liberty, the most powerful, it can be argued, has been the statue's link to European emigration.

Millions of women, men, and children, driven from their homelands by war, poverty, famine, and political oppression, came to the United States in a massive wave that lasted for several decades. Until 1892, immigrants arriving in New York Harbor were taken to Castle Garden, at the foot of Manhattan. But after 1892, when the immigration depot was opened at Ellis Island, next to the island where Liberty stood, the statue acquired an even deeper meaning for the millions of European immigrants who came to America's shores.

Imagine the effect that this colossal structure, the Statue of Liberty, must have had on those arriving in New York Harbor, seeking a new world and a new life! Liberty, after all, was the culmination of their hopes and dreams. For these refugees, who had lost or abandoned all that they once had had, who were exhausted from the ordeal of an extremely difficult ocean crossing, who were thrown together in confusion, speaking so many different languages, arrival in America seems to have been transfixed by Liberty's nurturing and protective visage—the very picture of strength, determination, and serenity.

The other element that explains Liberty's universal appeal is its rich, evocative imagery. The Statue of Liberty's symbolic strength exists apart from its status as a work of art. As distinguished art critic Harold Rosenberg once observed, "[T]he things that are important in a work of art and in a monument are not necessarily the same." It is therefore more worthwhile to probe the mystery of Liberty's appeal as a symbol than to evaluate the statue as a work of art. The aesthetic appeal of Liberty is not entirely the result of the formal structure; it also derives from the purely visual effects. To be sure, the physical fact of the statue is impressive. Yet of equal importance is the message that the Statue of Liberty expresses—in other words, what flows forth from her symbolically.

The thousands of transformations that the statue has under-

Fig. 5.3. "Liberty Feeding the World." This lithograph, an early-twentieth-century advertisement of a brand of cookies, "Famous Sea Foam Wafers," by the Holmes and Coutts Company of New York, depicts one of many product advertisements that have made use of the image of the Statue of Liberty. Reprinted by permission of Library of Congress, Washington, D.C.

gone at the whims of illustrators and cartoonists demonstrate the remarkable adaptability of Liberty's image to the multiplicity of causes with which it has been identified. Liberty, indeed, has proved to be a powerful catalyst for the human imagination (fig. 5.3).

Two anecdotes associated with the statue's creator, Frédéric-Auguste Bartholdi, and its builder, Emile Gaget, illustrate the range of symbolic and representational uses of Liberty's image. Bartholdi had taken pains to secure for himself all the legal rights to the design of the statue that he had created, thereby ensuring that he alone would hold the patent and reap the benefits from the future private and commercial uses of his design. His foresight paid off handsomely. Even before the official debut of the Statue of Liberty in October 1886, her image had been appropriated as a logo or insignia for every manner of business and commercial use.

Fig. 5.4. "Let the Advertising Agents Take Charge of the Bartholdi Business." This cartoon, from a *Puck* magazine of the early 1880s, caricatures the promotional interest of businesses in tying the image of Liberty to their products. However, the cartoon also reflects widespread concern about another issue—the difficulty in raising funds for the pedestal—and suggests the sale of advertising rights to the statue as a source of revenue. By the end of 1885, after an intense public relations drive, the public had responded sufficiently. Reprinted by permission of National Park Service, Statue of Liberty National Monument.

A *Puck* magazine cartoon of the early 1880s captures a double meaning in the commercialization of Liberty (fig. 5.4). At one level, the cartoon satirizes Bartholdi's instinct for the commercial value of his statue—and the hold that Liberty would exert on the popular imagination. At another level, however, the cartoon depicts a financial problem that nearly blocked the scheduled opening of the statue. Funds were in short supply for building the pedestal on which Liberty would stand; at the time, the statue consisted of hundreds of separate pieces, stored in crates, awaiting assembly. The cartoon hints at a solution to the funding shortage: raise money from businessmen by selling advertising rights for their products. Happily, by the end of 1885 sufficient funds had been raised to complete both the statue and its pedestal.

The other anecdote involves Emile Gaget, in whose Paris workshop the statue was constructed. For a trip to New York, it is said, Gaget packed a large number of miniature reproductions of Liberty, which he proceeded to sell and distribute. In French, Gaget's name is pronounced "ga-zhay," but in English, the name is pronounced "gadget," and he subsequently became identified with the small souvenirs and novelty devices that are now known as gadgets.

Both of these stories convey the Statue of Liberty's supple imagery and iconographic riches, which have been enjoyed by people in many different circumstances and walks of life.

Throughout Liberty's history, her image has been at times exalted, at other times exalting. At times she has seemed dynamic, at other times static. Liberty, it appears, has been buffeted not just by the harsh winds of New York Harbor but also by changing public moods and styles, by clashes of will and purpose, and by unpredictable events. Yet onlookers have insisted upon humanizing her, investing in her their concerns of the moment, appealing to her for relief and remedy, and transferring to her their wishes and hopes.

Alongside Liberty's unmatched adaptability is her timelessness, her superlative presence that seems to transcend any particular historical age, place, or set of events. Liberty's enduring quality derives also from the evocative nature of her pose. Her gesture of striding forward and holding high the torch of liberty has taken on a symbolic significance all its own. In this magnificent gesture the Statue of Liberty rises above the pettiness and parochialism of everyday life, above the limits of the human condition itself. The Statue of Liberty is, indeed, the supreme symbol for all those who refuse to accept the inevitability of fate and who cherish freedom.

NOTE

This essay is an adaptation of the address originally presented at the Cooper-Hewitt Colloquium, held on October 19, 1985.

BIBLIOGRAPHY

Blanchet, Christian, and Bertrand Dard. *Statue of Liberty: The First Hundred Years*. Translated from the French by Bernard A. Weisberger. New York: American Heritage Press, 1985.

Everybody's Gal

Women, Boundaries, and Monuments

BARBARA A. BABCOCK AND JOHN J. MACALOON

Women have entered into systems of representation only as the representation of something else, as justice, liberty, philosophy, or indeed some less abstract more human objectification of men's desire.
— JOANNA HODGE, Feminism and Post-Modernism

Woman is then the very ground of representation, both object and support of a desire which, intimately bound up with power and creativity, is the moving force of culture and history.
— TERESA DELAURETIS, Alice Doesn't

October 28, 1986, was the official centennial of the unveiling of the most famous female statue in the world. "Our fair lady" has been described as not only the most "prodigious structure of maternality" but also "the single most seductive structure" that Western man has ever erected.[1] She was, until the Russians raised their statue of the Motherland at Stalingrad after World War II, the world's largest female monument. In the words of one speaker at her 1886 debut, "Miss Liberty will always be the most beautiful lady in America."

Liberty's centennial birthday was a star-spangled extravaganza celebrated on the weekend of July 4, 1986—Independence Day.

79

New York City's mayor, Edward Koch, described the birthday party as "the best fireworks since Nero set Rome on fire." Lee Iacocca, who chaired a major fundraising effort, spoke earlier of the campaign to "get the lady out of trouble"—that is, re-dressed, face-lifted, and relighted through a two-year, $75 million makeover. The centennial events and the restoration of Liberty constitute a rationale for reexamining the concept-metaphor of woman in the dynamic of public culture-making, of the relationship between the body of woman and the body politic. While woman has frequently symbolized the *polis*, it is nonetheless a man-made and male-dominated body in which historical women have little place or voice.[2]

To put it in the broadest terms, the semiotic riot and the rhetoric of the last hundred years associated with the Statue of Liberty—especially that of the restoration and centennial—could not have happened if she were a he. The much-recounted 1980s narrative of deflowered and tarnished Liberty, violated by time and neglect, rescued by the white knight of corporate power and the people themselves, restored in a public ritual of renewal, purification, and rebirth, and celebrated in a palpably sexual way, is inconceivable without a female protagonist. American Express, for example, used the slogan "When did you first fall in love with her?" Moreover, the endless reproduction of the image is as dependent upon its gender as upon the miracles of modern technology.

Why, to paraphrase Marina Warner, are all these monuments maidens? If representation and reproduction are inseparable, is not woman always instrumental in the very discourse in which she is frequently displaced—the very ground of representation itself?[3] Women's bodies, through their use, consumption, and circulation, are the condition that makes social life and culture possible.[4] "Some concept of the sexed body is, therefore, essential to understanding social production, oppression, and resistance—a concept of the body as a socially inscribed, historically marked, psychically and interpersonally significant product."[5]

Men have not only excluded, ignored, and otherwise rendered women invisible, they have, for centuries, appropriated woman as a semiotic object and made her female form highly visible both to represent their established order and to subvert it. Whether to glorify civic and religious virtues or to undermine patriarchal structures, whether to personify Truth or Justice, Progress or Folly, a lot of cross-dressing has gone on in this and other cultures, much of it

Fig. 6.1. "USA Bonds. Weapons for Liberty." J. C. Leyendecker designed this poster, which celebrates the Boy Scouts and the role they played in the third Liberty Loan campaign, conducted during World War I. Reprinted by permission of National Park Service, Statue of Liberty National Monument.

on quite a staggering scale (fig. 6.1). "In male-dominated societies," Victor Turner once observed, "*communitas* may wear a skirt."[6] And what Victor Turner implies in alluding to the subversive power of the feminine, Bryan Turner makes explicit in his study *The Body and Society:* "Any discussion of social control must consider the control of women's bodies by men under a system of patriarchy."[7] Without the fetishized female, it is argued, the political economy of sovereign male selfhood would fall apart, for the distinguishing feature of the modern state is that it is the embodiment of representation, that it is fetishism writ large.[8]

The modern state is only the latest form to be implicated in such representations; their contemporary extension registers their temporal depth in European civilization. Western history began with the constitution of a boundary between Occident and Orient through the passage of symbolic women across it. So we are told by Herodotus, our first canonical historian. Phoenician traders abducted and raped the Argive princess Io, carrying her off to Egypt. In the Phoenician version, Herodotus notes, Io willingly bedded the foreign ship captain and left with the Asians to avoid discovery of her pregnancy. In revenge, Greeks abducted Europa, the daughter of the Phoenician king of Tyre, and after that, Medea, princess of Colchis. Inspired to take a role in this sexual project of political mapmaking, Paris next carried off Helen. But the Greeks spoiled the game by invading Asia to retrieve her. As Herodotus puts it:

> Up to this point it was only rape on both sides, one from the other; but from here on, say the Persians, the Greeks were greatly to blame. . . . "It is the work of unjust men, we think, to carry off women at all; but once they have been carried off, to take seriously the avenging of them is the part of fools, as it is the part of sensible men to pay no heed to the matter: clearly, the women would not have been carried off had they no mind to be."[9]

Rather than pronouncing on the truth or falsity of such "stories," Herodotus preferred to hurry on to verifiable political history, to Croesus, the first barbarian king "actually known" to have subdued Greeks into tribute. But the old story of sexualized political order and disorder refused to stay out of the new story of purely realistic, masculine power politics in the demarcation of Hellenes from Asians. With all the terms reversed, licit and illicit love instantly reappears with the account of Croesus's predecessor Candaules, who makes the barbarian error of "falling in love with his own wife" and of forcing his bodyguard Gyges to espy and attest to her naked beauty. Among these strange Asian others, "for even a man to be seen naked is an occasion of great shame,"[10] and discovering the offense, the queen (unnamed, therefore the grounding figure) offers Gyges the choice of death or of killing Candaules and wedding her and the throne. Choosing kingship, Gyges must send across the boundary to Greek Delphi to have his succession confirmed by Apollo's priestess against the violence of men disenfranchised by a regicide in defense of feminine marital chastity.

Transformation dogs transformation, but the structure remains intact, through Herodotus, the Greeks, and all Western cultural history, right into the realm of the modern nation-state and its sober political theory. Pallas Athena, the Virgin Mary, Marianne, the Motherland, the Statue of Liberty: wherever political, cultural, and moral boundaries require to be marked and at the same time trespassed, rigidified and liquidated, penetrated and incorporated, then symbolic women will be sent as gifts, betrothed, or abducted across those boundaries. But why, we might ask, following Erich Neumann's inquiry, do men construct such monuments and boundaries and what does such figurable libido mean? Why is the female body "a site on which masculine meanings get spoken and masculine desires enacted?"[11] For ourselves, Julia Kristeva answers that

> We live in a civilization in which the *consecrated* representation of femininity is subsumed under maternity. Under close examination, however, this maternity turns out to be an adult fantasy of a lost continent: what is involved, moreover, is not so much an idealized primitive mother as an idealization of the unlocalizable relationship between her and us, an idealization of primary narcissism.[12]

In that not fully delocalized yet still to us lost continent of Plato's *Symposium*, another answer is given. Political life and the female body have a common origin:

> With woman, a place can be found in political theory for both procreation and the representation of desire—and hence also the satisfaction of desire. Procreation and representation are related questions, moreover; taken together, they indicate the difficulty of conceptualizing, within a given political framework, the possibility of reproduction: reproduction of the real in order to satisfy desire, and reproduction of human life so that the city may endure.[13]

Time is the element in which human desire is elaborated and time is differentially conceived. In contrast to the linear temporality of history, which is perceived as masculine, both cyclical time and monumental time have been identified with women. Monumental time, the time of eternity, of continuity, is, Julia Kristeva argues, indissolubly linked with reproduction and, hence, with the representation of women.[14] In introducing his discussion of the Statue of Liberty, art historian Marvin Trachtenberg asks, "Just what makes a monument?"

> Monuments are public, permanent visual structures . . . that are
> intended to symbolize something generally shared by a group or
> even an entire society. . . . [M]onuments function as social mag-
> nets, crystallizations of social energy, one of the means civilization
> has devised to reinforce its cohesiveness and to give meaning and
> structure to life. Monuments are a way *men* transmit communal
> emotions, a medium of continuity and interaction between gener-
> ations, not only in space but across time, for to be monumental is
> to be permanent.[15]

But Trachtenberg fails to ask why *men's* ideals are so consistently
and so colossally embodied in female allegory, and he closes his
study with a pointed attack on feminist attempts to reinterpret and
reappropriate the symbol. This, he asserts, is "the most unthinking"
of innumerable exploitations of the statue because Liberty is, after
all, "immobilized and most heavily draped . . . idealized on a high
pedestal and put there by a whole crew of firm believers in the traditional arrangement between the sexes. Furthermore, not as we see
her, but as we know her, this decent woman takes on an altogether
different character—for a fee she is open to all for entry and exploration from below."[16]

"She is," President Reagan exclaimed on the occasion of her
second unveiling, "everybody's gal." Somewhat more analytically,
Kaja Silverman has remarked that "Liberty's interiority is a crucial
part of her artistic, psychic, and ideological functioning," permitting
the visitor to penetrate and be encompassed by a female body, while
simultaneously marveling at its enabling technology.[17]

Despite carefully chronicling the iconography of an idea,
Trachtenberg does not ask why Liberty has been eroticized as both
a goddess and a whore in Western culture at least since the Roman
Republic, or why the grandiose nationalistic self-glorifications of
the late nineteenth century in feats of technological prowess so frequently assumed a female form, or why the socially unfree were
used to symbolize freedom. The woman in the gift has escaped him.
As the suffragettes who circled Bedloe's Island in a boat at the dedication announced on a megaphone, if Liberty got down off her
pedestal, she would not have been allowed to vote in either France
or America—let alone attend her own unveiling ceremony. From
Virginia Woolf to Sherry Ortner, feminists have recognized the

imaginative, symbolic centrality of the socially and politically marginal, the hidden power of the virginal maternal complex in the symbolic economy of the West and the evolution of the nation-state. "Power in the West," Michel Foucault has observed, "is what displays itself the most, and thus what hides itself the best: what we have called 'political life' since the 19th century is the manner in which power presents its image. . . . Power is neither there, nor is that how it functions. The relations of power are perhaps among the best hidden things in the social body."[18]

Sherry Ortner suggests that the purity of women is "somehow structurally, functionally, and symbolically bound up with the historical emergence of systematically stratified state-type structures in the evolution of human society."[19] Julia Kristeva similarly argues that "the representation of virgin motherhood seems to have crowned society's efforts to reconcile survivals of matrilinearity and the unconscious needs of primary narcissism on the one hand with, on the other hand, the imperatives of the nascent exchange economy and, before long, of accelerated production, which required the addition of the superego and relied on the father's symbolic authority."[20]

With the Virgin Mary, Ortner argues, "the ideal woman emerges as all the best things at once, mother *and* virgin,"[21] and that complex is still very much with us in "Miss Liberty," "Mother of Exiles." Like the Virgin Mary, Liberty may be viewed as a masculine move simultaneously to control and co-opt the power of female sexuality, which is, Froma Zeitlin points out, indispensable for the continuity of the group but potentially disruptive in its free exercise.[22] Bryan Turner similarly argues that "the feminine body is the main challenge to continuity of property and power."[23] Women, therefore, "represent the necessity of the following challenge, which every city must meet despite the enormous risk involved: to make sure that time and desire, which threaten the political order, become its surest foundation."[24] Thus, Ortner contends, "male-defined structures represent and conceptualize their unity and status through the purity of their women."[25]

The France that gave us the virginal maternal Statue of Liberty to commemorate our Revolution personified its own revolution in the voluptuous figure of Marianne and painted Liberty, in Delacroix's *Liberty Leading the People*, as a bare-breasted virago lead-

ing the people to the barricades. As Catharine Gallagher has remarked in her insightful comments on Neil Hertz's discussion of
representation and sexuality in the French Revolution:

> From 1789 to 1870 French revolutionary violence repeatedly en-
> acted an ambivalent attack on patriarchy. And the emblematic im-
> portance of the uncontrolled and luridly sexual woman cannot be
> separated from that attack. On the one hand the revolutionaries
> needed to undermine the patriarchal assumptions that buttressed
> monarchial and aristocratic power. Thus the symbol of liberty
> who leads the people is female. But liberty, in the iconography of
> the age, often turns into a whore when she threatens the patriar-
> chal family as such. The sexually uncontrolled woman then be-
> comes a threat to all forms of property and established pow-
> er. . . . If the mother is not constrained then semiotic riot is the
> result. . . . Woman's biological power gives her the authority to
> call men's authorship into question.[26]

This ambivalence toward female sexuality and generativity and its
relationship to the subversion and disruption as well as the creation
and maintenance of the nation-state is reflected in the eighteenth-
century writings of two Frenchmen. Jean-Jacques Rousseau, in his
Politics and the Arts, proclaimed that "never has a people perished
from an excess of wine; all perish from the disorder of women."[27]
The other, Michel-Guillaume-Jean de Crèvecoeur, in his *Letters
from an American Farmer*, explained that one "becomes an American
by being received in the broad lap of our great *Alma Mater*. Here
individuals of all nations are melted into a new race of men."[28] He
also remarked, "[I]f anyone asks me what I think the chief cause of
the extraordinary prosperity and growing power of this nation, I
should answer it is due to the superiority of their women." As the
Frenchman gives birth to American society's master metaphor for
itself, "Woman" as sign and "women" as historical agents are at
once registered, confounded, and elided in the generation of "real"
power and prosperity.

Given these divergent eighteenth-century configurations, how
better for nineteenth-century Frenchmen to symbolically and
retroactively contain semiotic chaos, to domesticate revolution,
than to monumentally reinterpret Liberty as a chaste mother for
their "sister republic"? But one does not give away one's mother.

Shared matrilineal filiation first requires a wedding. Between her conversion from revolutionary virago to chaste matriarch at home and her installation as virgin mother of America (and her ensuing career of promiscuity there), Liberty had to pass as a bride across the Atlantic. As beloved daughter of France, she was given in marriage to the foreigners. Adjudicating, pacifying, and recontrolling boundaries by wife-giving across them is another perpetual motif in European cultural history, the alternative to invasion and rapine by others, or, worse, the treachery of daughters' willful desires for foreigners. By offering Liberty, France sought to remind America of its junior and dependent status, while domesticating the upstart nation's newly threatening powers. By accepting the gift as instead a species of tribute, America sought to remind France that the Woman, her libertine fires, and her progeny had long since passed over by their own accord.

A "longer since," of course, involved rapacious conquest by European males, across the ocean and into the body of the new continent. As Annette Kolodny has pointed out in *The Lay of the Land*, what was done from the sixteenth century on to the land that was to become both the referent and the recipient of Liberty, "this stupendous specimen of womanhood," was literally as well as metaphorically a bold exercise of masculine power over the feminine—a feminine that was experienced at once as mother and virgin, the object of filial homage and erotic desire, a space of rebirth as well as one to be penetrated and conquered. European explorers and artists initially portrayed America as a dusky aboriginal female accompanied by tropical fauna and cornucopias of abundance—an image of exotica and erotica, of untold treasure and pleasure waiting to be ravaged.[29] By the early nineteenth century, this wild woman had metamorphosed into a plumed Greek goddess of Liberty who became interchangeable with Columbia, a more mature and dignified female representing the political body of the nation (fig. 6.2).[30]

Thus transformed, enlarged, and ennobled, Liberty was fitted for a role in another transformation of "Woman" in Indo-European political thought—the mythos, famous since Sir James George Frazer, of the Invader-King. Marshall Sahlins comments:

> The legends of the Latin kings from Romulus to the second Tarquin, as the Greeks from Tantalus and Pelops to Agamemnon, show consistent similarities in the philosophy of polity. The king

Fig. 6.2. A cigar box label depicting America as Indian Maiden, as Liberty, and as Columbia. Source: Collection of Jeffrey Eger. Reprinted by permission of Visions Photo, Inc., New York City.

is an outsider, often a warrior prince whose father is a god or king of his native land. But, exiled by his love of power or banished for murder, the hero is unable to succeed there. Instead he takes power in another place, and *through a woman:* princess of the native people whom he gains by a miraculous exploit involving feats of strength, ruse, rape, athletic prowess, and/or the murder of his predecessor.[31]

From the perspective of the conquered, however, it is through that encompassing woman that the invader's powers are domesticated by being married in. Thereafter, they are indigenous powers. Far from having disappeared in enlightened modern society, such "primitive" political thought stands everywhere unnoticed in such figures as Liberty and the discourses surrounding her.[32] The historical conquistadores and colonizers, rapists of the American land, have themselves been incorporated through the magical powers of her melting pot. Her maternal guardianship of democratic liberty and the desire it is said to promiscuously spawn among all peoples of the world ensure that America will never be violently invaded again. One of the highlights of the year-long quincentenary celebration of Christopher Columbus's "encounter with America" was a Las Vegas wedding by satellite on Saint Valentine's Day between the Statue of Liberty and Barcelona's statue of Columbus. Catalans and Americans who scoffed at this tasteless showbiz failed to appreciate its sophisticated understanding of political truth.

Bartholdi's image of Liberty Enlightening the World was a revision of his Egypt Bringing the Light to Asia, or Progress, a sending of Europa home, we might say. He had proposed this colossal female figure holding a torch as a lighthouse to be raised at the entrance to the Suez Canal, another French engineering feat. Despite his disavowals of any connection, the figures and models he constructed after seeing New York Harbor in 1871 and being awed both by the natural grandeur and by the technological accomplishments of America bear striking resemblance to this earlier woman. Bartholdi also went to great lengths to dissociate his Liberty from the revolutionary emotion of Delacroix's image. In contrast to that dangerously disorderly, half-naked woman, Laboulaye insisted in his 1876 fundraising speech, "This Liberty will not be the one wearing a red bonnet on her head, a pike in her hand, who walks on corpses. It will be the Liberty who does not hold an incendiary torch, but a beacon which enlightens!"[33]

In the statement that had originally inspired Bartholdi many years earlier, Laboulaye imaged Liberty not as chaotic and destructive but as nurturing and maternal: "Liberty is the mother of a family who watches over the cradle of her children." Between them, Bartholdi and Laboulaye produced a monumental and controlled syncretic female combining (1) the classical iconography of Faith, Truth, and Liberty without the Phrygian cap that had become the inflammatory *bonnet rouge* of the French Revolution, crowned instead with the rays of the sun god Helios; (2) the imagery of freemasonry; (3) the inspiration of the Colossus of Rhodes; and (4) a mother fixation. In the process they transformed Liberty from a grotesque revolutionary body into a classical and aristocratic one that would tower above what poet Emma Lazarus memorialized as "huddled masses" and "wretched refuse."[34]

Bartholdi referred to his sculpture variously as his "big girl," his "daughter Liberty," "his American." Although some sources claim that Bartholdi never revealed the influences in shaping the Statue of Liberty, one source attributes to him the following characterization of the statue's image:

> Make the statue a woman because the symbol for Liberty has always been a woman. Women often represent great ideas. The torch is the symbol of freedom. It lights the way for people who love Liberty. The seven rays of her crown will enlighten the seven seas and the seven continents. Use mother, Charlotte as a model for her face. Mother's face shows strength and suffering. Model the statue's arms after my fiancée's beautiful arms. Give her clothes from ancient Greece, the birthplace of democracy. Make her walk forward to show her progress toward freedom. The date of American Independence, July 4, 1776, will be on the tablet. The broken chains at her feet will show her escaping from bondage. Make her really huge! Liberty is a big idea![35]

Obviously, he succeeded, for "what Bartholdi's statue held out to his compatriots was the promise of a liberty uncontaminated by passion, a republic without republicanism, and a political arena from which the female body would be discreetly barred." But, despite this foreclosure of sexuality and resanctification of motherhood, the other persistent rumor that has circulated with respect to Liberty's origin is that her model was a prostitute. And, given the reality that, as Trachtenberg has observed, "for a fee she is open to all for entry and exploration," it is possible to view Liberty as a prostitute, although she seems to be a mother. One can, however, as Kaja Silverman observes, return to this phantasmic mother's body "without having to confront her sexuality in any way."[36]

She was not finished in time for the centennial proper, so the disembodied right arm holding the torch was sent for the Philadelphia celebration. Two years later her head was displayed at the Paris Universal Exposition of 1878. The fetishization of body parts did not end even there. When work had been completed to just below the statue's thigh in July 1882, Bartholdi invited the press to a luncheon inside Liberty's right knee, which forty editors and correspondents attended. On the other side of the Atlantic, the American press was far less enthusiastic and sympathetic; as Bartholdi had predicted, "[T]he greatest difficulty will be with the American character."[37] While the dissembled Liberty waited in France, Americans were ambivalent and anything but organized in preparing a berth for this "pagan goddess," which many regarded as yet another gesture of French cultural imperialism. Those offered a bride were slow to answer the invitation. Society architect Richard Morris Hunt was engaged to design the pedestal, but neither wealthy benefactors nor the government came forward to support the project, and far from enough funds were available to erect it.

The Lee Iacocca of the 1880s was Joseph Pulitzer, a Hungarian Jewish immigrant who used his newly acquired *New York World* to embarrass Americans into contributing, appropriated the statue as his masthead, made her the people's woman, and raised both the money and the circulation of his newspaper to the largest in the Western Hemisphere. On March 15, 1885, Pulitzer made his famous appeal:

> Money must be raised to complete the pedestal for the Bartholdi statue. It would be an ineffaceable disgrace to New York City and the American Republic to have France send us this splendid gift without our having provided even so much as a landing place for it. . . . [T]here is but one thing that can be done. We must raise the money. . . . [T]he $250,000 that the making of the Statue cost was paid in by the masses of the French people—by the working men, the tradesmen, the shopgirls, the artisans—by all, irrespective of class or condition. Let us respond in like manner. Let us not wait for the millionaires to give the money . . . [T]ake this appeal to yourself personally. It is meant for every reader of THE WORLD. Give something, however little, send it to us. . . . We will publish the name of every giver, however small the sum given. Let us hear from the people.[38]

The response was overwhelming. With their pennies, nickels, and dimes, the American people signaled their acceptance of the French gift and made the alien goddess an image of themselves, of the social collectivity. Thus, as Kaja Silverman points out, France's gift was semiotically reconstituted as a representation no longer of "French political aspirations, but of the American socius." Pulitzer's intervention "created a situation where the work of art functioned to gratify the 'imperishable' desire for social collectivity while at the same time succumbing irretrievably to sign-value and commodification. . . . The American public was sold the image of the United

States in which they dreamed of seeing themselves, and they have continued to pay for that dream ever since."[39]

Proclaimed a national monument in 1924, this phantasmic mother signifying freedom, America, and hope for the "children" has, as the preceding implies, been the subject of endless veneration, commercialization, and satire. The "bearer of a million dreams," she is an extremely multivocal and fluid key symbol, who has had a changing and intense relationship with American history and experience. The reinterpretations and uses of the lady are so numerous and various as to defy compilation, and the trafficking in her image reached epic proportions during the restoration and the centennial, surpassed perhaps only by centuries of Mariolatry. Liberty has become, as a 1986 postcard announced, the "All-American Cover Girl."

The victim of what one commentator aptly called "statuary rape," her dignity has been sorely tried in the name of raising money to repair the ravages of time and to celebrate her birthday.[40] Whether as a centennial VISA card or a Liberty version of Trivial Pursuit, one could literally use her in 1986 as an item of exchange and a means of conspicuous consumption—women, goods, and symbols all at once. The aforementioned items are among the "official" reproductions of her image licensed by the centennial commission, which also approved the recycling of her flesh. During her monumental face-lift and body wrap, the lady shed a hundred tons of scrap metal, which was reshaped into Iacocca-endorsed relics. For prices ranging from $10 to $300, one could "have a piece of the actual lady." For even less money, one could purchase Styrofoam significata. And, for ambitious hobbyists, a "Build your own Statue of Liberty" kit could be purchased for $7.95, tweezers, glue, and toothpicks not included.

Such commodification and the coupling of Lady Liberty with Lady Luck is not, however, an American invention of the 1980s. As Nancy Fox points out in her fine illustrated history of America's imaging of Liberty, we have been "taking liberties with Liberty" for more than two centuries. To raise money for her construction, Bartholdi himself organized a lottery, made two hundred replicas, and licensed her image to French businesses. By now, she is surely the prime inhabitant of the Garage Sale Hall of Fame and has become (if she has not always been), in the words of a *New Republic* editor, "a high-priced corporate tart." There is little that this ultimate

American icon has not been used to sell, from millions of sparklers to $15 billion worth of World War I Liberty Bonds to breath freshener, for those who truly want to breathe free. She has become the ultimate commodity, able to "float," as they say, any number of products.[41]

There have, for example, been endless substitutions in the syntagma of "Liberty enlightening the world"—many, of course, in the direction of female activities. One of our favorites is "Liberty cleaning the world"—a turn-of-the-century advertisement for Soapine the Dirt Killer. And lest one think things have really changed, Ajax cleanser used the statue in a 1990 ad. An 1880 ad for Brainerd and Armstrong silk thread predated the erection of the statue and anticipated commodification in the direction of women's work. And, there are countless "Liberty" brands using the name as well as the image. The most famous is probably Liberty Mutual Insurance Company, which gives us a "wall of protection."

A "woman for all seasons," Liberty has inspired hundreds of artists, starred in movies and musicals, and been the subject of folk art in many media. She has been appropriated by various causes, used to make radically different political statements from the far left to the extreme right, and been the site of public demonstrations since 1926. She has also engendered countless cartoons, jokes, and parodies, which the centennial both occasioned and reassembled; one example is a tiny flip-the-pages book titled *The Statue of Liberty Takes a Dive*—a cartoon of Liberty tossing away her torch, crown, and robe, diving off her pedestal, and cavorting naked in the water. Or, one of several terrible jokes circulating in the summer of 1986, "Did you hear that the Statue of Liberty has AIDS? She caught it from the Staten Island Ferry." Equally offensive is one of the first political cartoons that appeared in 1884, even before the statue did. Titled "Barsqualdi's Liberty Frightening the World, Bedbugs Island, NY," this Currier and Ives print showed a black woman carrying a book of port charges for New York Harbor. It was feared at the time that the proposed port charges would divert shipping from the city in favor of less expensive ports. Clearly, the influx of what many regarded as undesirable immigrants was anticipated and feared as well, invader-populations replacing invader-kings. In an 1890 cartoon against immigration from *Judge* magazine, Liberty tells Treasury Secretary William Windom, "If you're going to turn this island into a garbage dump, I'm going back to France."

In World War II even more than World War I, the statue became *the* symbol of patriotism, the nation's feminine complement to masculine affairs of state. She was everywhere and everything that was being fought for. It was then that she became, as Reagan has reminded us, "everybody's gal." And it was after World War II that the Boy Scouts sold eight-foot replicas across the country. Conversely, the unpopularity of the Vietnam War was also inscribed on her body, as in Tomi Ungerer posters depicting Vietnamese being forced to "eat" a Statue of Liberty and to "kiss" her bare buttocks. That was neither the first nor the last time that Liberty appeared unfavorably. She was the negative subject of countless cartoons in 1984 when a sweep of illegal aliens was initiated. Recently, she became the "Statue of Litter" in a cartoon that appeared several times in New Mexico newspapers in a vain attempt to keep that state from becoming the "landfill of enchantment."

Noting such uses and abuses, many commentators have remarked that the Statue of Liberty remains a powerful and treasured symbol *despite* the liberties that have been taken with her image. Michael Thompson-Noel's remarks in an August 1986 number of London's *Financial Times* are a case in point: "Although Miss Liberty has been exploited and vulgarized with endearing crassness for the whole of her first century, she remains one of the great symbols of refuge and optimism." Conversely, we would argue that she is a powerful symbol precisely *because* of the ways she can be used. Such irreverence is quintessentially American, essentially woman, and perhaps the most significant embodiment of all of freedom—"the freedom to create anything you want, anytime, anywhere."[42] It is precisely because Liberty provides this phantasmic image through which America constitutes itself as a social aggregation that she has become such a valuable and multivalent commodity.

Clearly, we cannot control the traffic in women, and it is obviously futile to struggle against female objectification, but we can do something about the interpretation thereof, such as examining the politics and psychodynamics of a patriarchal symbolic order and reviewing political allegory and its female embodiment in the context of a structural history of the Western political imagination. Is not eroticism inevitable? Can the political deployment of a feminine icon now escape a pornographic structure?[43] How is Liberty as woman related to the creation and maintenance of the nation-state, as well as its subversion and disruption?[44] Until such systems of meaning and signification are questioned and understood, women's bodies will remain the objects of male definition and scrutiny, appropriated and used to reproduce state power from the nation's resources, yet disavowed in the bodies politic to which history has given birth.

NOTES

Portions of this essay were originally published in Barbara A. Babcock, "Taking Liberties, Writing from the Margins, and Doing It with a Difference," *Journal of American Folklore* 100 (1987): 390–411.

1. Unless otherwise noted, the preceding and other quoted statements describing Liberty were made by unidentified commentators in a variety of magazines and popular publications occasioned by the centennial. See, for example, the special issues listed in the bibliography.

2. Gatens, "Toward a Feminist Philosophy of the Body."

3. Ibid.; deLauretis, *Alice Doesn't.*

4. Irigaray, *This Sex Which Is Not One,* 171.

5. Gross, "Philosophy, Subjectivity, and the Body," 140.

6. Victor W. Turner, "Comments and Conclusions," 289.

7. Bryan S. Turner, *The Body and Society,* 3.

8. Lechte, *Julia Kristeva,* 150.

9. Herodotus, *The History,* bk. 1, chap. 4.

10. Ibid., bk. 1, chap. 10.

11. Ruthven, *Feminist Literary Studies,* 45.

12. Kristeva, "Stabat Mater," 99.

13. Plato's *Symposium,* quoted in Canto, "The Politics of Women's Bodies," 340.

14. Kristeva, "Women's Time," 31–36.

15. Trachtenberg, *The Statue of Liberty,* 7. Emphasis added.

16. Ibid., 196.

17. Silverman, "Liberty, Maternity, Commodification," 83.

18. Quoted in Kritzman, *Michel Foucault, Politics, Philosophy, Culture,* 118.

19. Ortner, "The Virgin and the State," 23.

20. Kristeva, "Stabat Mater," 115.

21. Ortner, "Virgin and State," 26.

22. Zeitlin, "The Dynamics of Misogyny," 158.

23. Bryan Turner, *Body and Society*, 37.

24. Canto, "Politics of Women's Bodies," 349.

25. Ortner, "Virgin and State," 22.

26. Gallagher, Fineman, and Hertz, "More about 'Medusa's Head,'" 56–57.

27. Quoted in Pateman, "'The Disorder of Women,'" 20.

28. Quoted in Kolodny, *The Lay of the Land*, 26.

29. Green, "The Pocahontas Perplex."

30. On the imaging of America as an Indian princess, see Green, "Pocahontas Perplex"; Tiffany and Adams, *The Wild Woman*; and Fox, *Liberties with Liberty*, for discussion and illustration of early iconography. For further discussion of the other female forms, such as Columbia, in which America was embodied, see Fox, *Liberties with Liberty*, and Warner, *Monuments and Maidens*.

31. Sahlins, *Islands of History*, 81–82.

32. MacAloon, *Brides of Victory*.

33. Quoted in Spiering, *Bearer of a Million Dreams*, 69.

34. See Trachtenberg, *Statue of Liberty*, for elaboration of the syncretic iconography of Bartholdi's Liberty. For further discussion of the imaging of revolution in Republican France, see Agulhon, *Marianne into Battle*; and Ozouf, *Festivals and the French Revolution*.

35. Quoted in *The Kids' Official Statue of Liberty Magazine*, 13.

36. Silverman, "Liberty, Maternity, Commodification," 75, 82.

37. Quoted in Spiering, *Bearer of a Million Dreams*, 30.

38. Ibid., 162.

39. Silverman, "Liberty, Maternity, Commodification," 75–76.

40. Davenport, "Statuary Rape," 32–33.

41. For further discussion of the commodification of Liberty and the corporate takeover of her restoration, see Gratz and Fettmann, "The Selling of Miss Liberty," and Silverman, "Liberty, Maternity, Commodification."

42. Fox, *Liberties with Liberty*, 18.

43. Hunt, *Eroticism and the Body Politic.*

44. See Agulhon, *Marianne into Battle*, and Warner, *Monuments and Maidens*, for further discussion of the changing representations and political uses of Liberty and her problematic and essential ambiguity.

BIBLIOGRAPHY

Agulhon, Maurice. *Marianne into Battle: Republican Imagery and Symbolism in France, 1789–1880.* Cambridge: Cambridge University Press, 1981.

Allen, Leslie. *Liberty: The Statue and the American Dream.* New York: Statue of Liberty–Ellis Island Foundation, 1985.

Babcock, Barbara A. "Taking Liberties, Writing from the Margins, and Doing It with a Difference." *Journal of American Folklore* 100 (1987): 390–411.

Berlant, Lauren. "America, Post-Utopia: Body, Landscape, and National Fantasy in Hawthorne's *Native Land.*" *Arizona Quarterly* 44, no. 4 (1989): 14–54.

Canto, Monique. "The Politics of Women's Bodies: Reflections on Plato." In *The Female Body in Western Culture: Contemporary Perspectives*, edited by Susan Rubin Suleiman, 339–53. Cambridge, Mass.: Harvard University Press, 1986.

Cowan, Michael. "Competing for Liberty: The Political Culture of 'National' Celebrations." Paper presented at the Celebrating American Public Culture Symposium of the American Studies Association Convention, New York, November 23, 1987.

Davenport, Rattan. "Statuary Rape." *Social Anarchism* 13 (1987): 32–33.

deLauretis, Teresa. *Alice Doesn't: Feminism, Semiotics, Cinema.* Bloomington: Indiana University Press, 1984.

Fox, Nancy Jo. *Liberties with Liberty: The Fascinating History of America's Proudest Symbol.* New York: E. P. Dutton, 1985.

Gallagher, Catharine, Joel Fineman, and Neil Hertz. "More about 'Medusa's Head.'" *Representations* 3 (1983): 55–72.

Gatens, Moira. "Toward a Feminist Philosophy of the Body." In *Crossing Boundaries: Feminisms and the Critique of Knowledges*, edited by Barbara Caine, E. A. Grosz, and Marie de Lepervanche, 59–70. Sydney, Australia: Allen and Unwin, 1988.

Gratz, Roberta Brandes, and Eric Fettmann. "The Selling of Miss Liberty." *Nation* 241, no. 15 (1985): 465–76.

Green, Rayna. "The Pocahontas Perplex: The Image of Indian Women in American Culture." *Massachusetts Review* 16, no. 4 (1976): 698–714.

Gross, Elizabeth. "Philosophy, Subjectivity, and the Body: Kristeva and Irigaray." In *Feminist Challenges: Social and Political Theory*, edited by Carole Pateman and Elizabeth Gross, 124–43. Boston: Northeastern University Press, 1987.

Grumet, Michael. *Images of Liberty*. New York: Arbor House, 1986.

"Hail, Liberty!" *Time* 128, no. 2 (July 14, 1986).

Heffernan, Maureen. *The Statue of Liberty: A History and Celebration*. Minneapolis: Woodbury Press, 1986.

Herodotus. *The History*. Translated by David Grene. Chicago: University of Chicago Press, 1987.

Hertz, Neil. "Medusa's Head: Male Hysteria under Political Pressure." *Representations* 4 (1983): 27–54.

Hodge, Joanna. "Feminism and Post-Modernism: Misleading Divisions Imposed by the Opposition between Modernism and Post-Modernism." In *The Problem of Modernity: Adorno and Benjamin*, edited by Andrew Benjamin, 86–111. London: Routledge, 1989.

Hunt, Lynn, ed. *Eroticism and the Body Politic*. Baltimore: Johns Hopkins University Press, 1991.

Irigaray, Luce. *This Sex Which Is Not One*. Ithaca, N.Y.: Cornell University Press, 1985.

———. *Speculum of the Other Woman*. Ithaca, N.Y.: Cornell University Press, 1985.

The Kids' Official Statue of Liberty Magazine. New York: Lorimar Telepictures Publications, 1986.

Kolodny, Annette. *The Lay of the Land: Metaphor as Experience and History in American Life and Letters*. Chapel Hill: University of North Carolina Press, 1975.

Kristeva, Julia. "Stabat Mater." In *The Female Body in Western Culture: Contemporary Perspectives*, edited by Susan Rubin Suleiman, 99–118. Cambridge, Mass.: Harvard University Press, 1986.

———. "Women's Time." In *Feminist Theory: A Critique of Ideology*, edited by Nannerl O. Keohane, Michelle Z. Rosaldo, and Barbara C. Gelpi, 31–53. Chicago: University of Chicago Press, 1982.

Kritzman, Lawrence D., ed. *Michel Foucault, Politics, Philosophy, Culture: Interviews and Other Writings, 1977–1984*. New York: Routledge, 1990.

Lechte, John. *Julia Kristeva*. London: Routledge, 1990.

"Liberty at 100." *Life* 9, no. 7 (July 1986).

MacAloon, John J. *Brides of Victory: Nationalism and Gender in Olympic Ritual*. London: Berg Publishers, in press.

Murray, Timothy. "Subliminal Libraries: Showing Lady Liberty and Documenting Death." *Discourse* 9 (1987): 107–24.

National Geographic. July 1986. Washington: National Geographic Society.

Neumann, Erich. *The Great Mother: An Analysis of the Archetype*. Princeton,

Neumann, Erich. *The Great Mother: An Analysis of the Archetype*. Princeton, N.J.: Princeton University Press, 1963.

Ortner, Sherry B. "The Virgin and the State." *Feminist Studies* 4, no. 3 (1978): 19–35.

Our Liberty. Special Issue, *New York* 19, no. 19 (May 12, 1986).

Ozouf, Mona. *Festivals and the French Revolution*. Cambridge, Mass.: Harvard University Press, 1988.

Pateman, Carole. "'The Disorder of Women': Women, Love, and the Sense of Justice." *Ethics* 91, no. 1 (1980): 20–34.

Robbins, Peggy. "The Most Beautiful Lady in America." *American History Illustrated* 19, no. 6 (1984): 30–37.

Ruthven, K. K. *Feminist Literary Studies: An Introduction*. Cambridge: Cambridge University Press, 1984.

Sahlins, Marshall. *Islands of History*. Chicago: University of Chicago Press, 1985.

Silverman, Kaja. "Liberty, Maternity, Commodification." *New Formations* 5 (1988): 69–90.

Spiering, Frank. *Bearer of a Million Dreams: The Biography of the Statue of Liberty*. Ottawa: M. Jameson Books, 1986.

Sweet Land of Liberty. Special Issue, *Newsweek* 107, no. 22A (Summer 1986).

Tiffany, Sharon W., and Kathleen J. Adams. *The Wild Woman: An Inquiry into the Anthropology of an Idea*. Cambridge, Mass.: Schenkman Publishing Company, 1985.

Trachtenberg, Marvin. *The Statue of Liberty*. New York: Penguin, 1986.

Turner, Bryan S. *The Body and Society: Explorations in Social Theory*. Oxford: Basil Blackwell, 1984.

Turner, Victor W. "Comments and Conclusions." In *The Reversible World: Symbolic Inversion in Art and Society*, edited by Barbara A. Babcock, 276–96. Ithaca, N.Y.: Cornell University Press, 1978.

Warner, Marina. *Monuments and Maidens: The Allegory of Female Form*. New York: Atheneum, 1985.

Weinbaum, Paul. *Statue of Liberty: Heritage of America*. Las Vegas: K. C. Publications, 1979.

Weisberger, Bernard A. *Statue of Liberty: The First Hundred Years*. New York: American Heritage, 1985.

Zeitlin, Froma. "The Dynamics of Misogyny: Myth and Mythmaking in *The Oresteia*." *Arethusa* 11, nos. 1–2 (1978): 149–84.

Chinese Perspectives

EDITORS' NOTE: The essay and the interview that follow present two Chinese perspectives on the ideals of freedom and democracy that the Statue of Liberty has symbolized for peoples throughout the world. The first, "A Beijing Chronicle," was written by Tsao Hsingyuan, a sculptor, art historian, and Asian specialist who now resides in California. Tsao was a witness when the Goddess of Democracy, a statue resembling the Statue of Liberty, was created by art students in Beijing, China. A symbol of the student-based pro-democracy movement that arose in China in 1989, the statue stood for five days in Beijing's Tiananmen Square. A brief version of her essay was published in the *Los Angeles Times* of June 18, 1989. The second perspective, "Chinese Views of Liberty, Democracy, and the Pursuit of Scientific Knowledge," arises out of an interview with Professor Fang Li Zhi, an internationally famous physicist who also is one of China's leading advocates of human rights and democracy. Professor Fang, now teaching at the University of Arizona in Tucson, offers his experiences and reflections on the prospects for freedom and democracy in the People's Republic of China and on the aspirations of the Chinese people. Dr. Fang also examines the close relationship between freedom and the pursuit of scientific knowledge. He compares his experiences in China with his experiences in the United States, where he has lived since 1990. The interview with Professor Fang occurred in two parts, on February 1, 1992, and April 2, 1992.

A BEIJING CHRONICLE, BY TSAO HSINGYUAN

Nothing excites a sculptor as much as seeing a work of her own creation take shape. This time, however, I was watching the creation of a sculpture that I had no part in making and feeling the same excitement. It was the Goddess of Democracy statue that stood for five days in Tiananmen Square, from May 30 to the morning of June 4, 1989 (fig. 7.1). The Goddess became the most prominent symbol of the student movement for democracy that during a brief period stirred the hopes of the Chinese people and captured the imagination of peoples throughout the world. I witnessed the making of it and want to put the story on record.

I myself was until July 1988 a graduate student at the Central Academy of Fine Arts in Beijing, where the sculpture was made, and was living there when these events took place. Since I was trained as a sculptor before becoming an art historian, I have been especially close to the faculty and students of the Central Academy's sculpture department, and I was looked on by the students as a kind of older sister. I did not participate directly in the making of the statue because I was married to an American professor and was living mostly abroad. It could have brought trouble to the students if I had taken part. So I avoided conspicuous involvement, adopting the role of observer and supportive friend.

By May 27, a week after the declaration of martial law in Beijing, the student movement for democracy seemed to be losing some of its momentum. The students suspected that the government was waiting for them to get tired and leave the square by their own choice. Word got around, however, that on the evening of May 29 there would be an "important announcement" on the Central Broadcasting station; it was expected to be the resignation of Zhao Ziyang [chairman of China's Communist party]. The Federation of Beijing University Students, which was coordinating the democracy movement, decided to respond to this broadcast by staging the largest demonstration of all, involving students, workers, and residents of Beijing. The student federation made plans to leave behind in Tiananmen Square a monumental work of art that would symbolize the democratic ideal so long as the artwork would be allowed to stand.

Students and faculty of the Central Academy of Fine Arts, which is located only a short distance from Tiananmen Square, had

Fig. 7.1. Goddess of Democracy. For five days in 1989, a ten-meter-high statue made of Styrofoam plastic and plaster stood in Tiananmen Square in Beijing, the capital of the People's Republic of China. In this photograph, taken by Pat Benic on May 30, the Goddess of Democracy faces a huge portrait of late Chinese leader Mao Tse-tung. Also shown are participants in the student-led pro-democracy demonstrations for which the statue was a rallying symbol. The protest was crushed by the Chinese army, and the statue was destroyed. Reprinted by permission of Reuters/Bettmann.

been actively involved in the student demonstrations from the beginning. A representative of the student federation came to the Central Academy to ask the students to produce a large-scale work of art, a statue that could be ready by the time of the planned demonstration on May 30. That gave the art students three days in which to do it. The federation offered 8,000 yuan (more than $2,000 U.S. by the official rate) for materials and other expenses. Fifteen undergraduate students in the Central Academy's sculpture department, all young men in their early twenties, agreed to take on the job.

The student federation suggested that the sculpture be a replica of the Statue of Liberty in New York. A small reproduction of the Statue of Liberty had been carried in a procession by demonstrators in Shanghai two days earlier. But the sculpture students rejected that idea because it might be viewed as too openly pro-American and because the copying of an existing work was contrary to their principles as creative artists. They also rejected a suggestion of a "Chinese-style" work, because there is no tradition in China for sculpture that expresses a political concept, apart from the Communist revolutionary sculptures, which would not have been appropriate. To do a statue in the manner of Buddhist cave sculpture might have been pleasing to foreign viewers but would have sacrificed the emotional impact that a statue symbolizing democracy was to have on the great mass of people for whom it was made.

What was called for, the students felt, was a new work of universal appeal, Chinese only in the eclectic way that today's China borrows what it needs from other cultures. But apart from style, the students had another problem: the short time in which they had to complete it. How could an original and monumental work of sculpture be finished in three days' time, even if they worked through the night? Normally, a longer period of time is needed, first to create a model and then to make the finished work.

Their solution was ingenious and explains some features of the statue as it took shape: its slightly off-balance look and its posture with two arms raised to hold up a torch, whereas the Statue of Liberty uses only one arm. The students, with the strong academic training that young artists receive in China, seized upon a thoroughly academic solution to their problem. They decided to save time by adapting for their purpose a studio practice work that one of them (or perhaps it was several of them) had already made—a half-meter-high clay sculpture of a man grasping a pole with two raised hands and leaning his weight on it. This model had been done originally to demonstrate how the distribution of weight is affected when the center of gravity is shifted outside a subject, but it had now become the unlikely beginning from which the Goddess of Democracy was to evolve. The students cut off the lower part of the pole and added a torch at the top. They leaned the sculpture into a more upright position, and they changed the man's face on the original model into a woman's, also adding breasts and long hair.

The students sought to portray the Goddess of Democracy as a healthy young woman, for which Chinese sculpture tradition offered no models. They did have available, however, an image from a work of art of the Soviet school of revolutionary realism, a work by female sculptor Vera Mukhina, whose monumental statue "A Worker and Collective Farm Woman," originally placed atop the Soviet Pavilion at the 1937 Paris World's Fair, is still much admired in

China. The face of the farm woman became the inspiration for the face of the Goddess of Democracy.

This is how a half-meter-high statue of a man became transformed into a ten-meter-high statue of a goddess.

The statue was divided into four horizontal sections, and teams of young sculptors transferred the measurements of these, by a process well known to academic sculptors, to the corresponding parts of the huge work that would be assembled in Tiananmen Square. The material used was Styrofoam plastic, a material rarely used before in China for monumental sculpture. Large blocks of it were carved into rough approximations of the shapes desired and then wired together, with plaster added to the surface to join the pieces together more strongly and to allow for finer modeling.

The Goddess of Democracy had no single creator or artist. It was as close to a truly collaborative work as any project of this kind can be. Among the group of fifteen or so undergraduate students who designed and built it, a smaller number emerged naturally as leaders to plan the operation and coordinate the work shifts. One group of sculptors would work while others slept.

One young Central Academy faculty member, openly supportive of the students, served as a go-between to help them get materials and tools that they could not otherwise have obtained. Others on the faculty offered support behind the scenes, persuading the political leaders in the academy to protect the students. Without their help, the sculpture could not have been made openly in the sculpture department's outdoor workspace within the Central Academy compound.

The Goddess of Democracy that stood in Tiananmen Square was built in the academy courtyard, where other large-scale sculptures had been made. Teachers living in the buildings surrounding it complained that they could not sleep because of the noise, since the work continued through the night and there were always onlookers, commenting and talking. The academy's overt attitude toward the making of the sculpture was one of passive toleration, not active sanction; that was impossible. But many of the faculty, perhaps most, approved quietly, and when the statue was moved to the square, many of them went along to show support.

When the time came to move the pieces of the statue to Tiananmen Square, another problem arose. The students had intended to transport the statue in one of the academy's trucks, but the State Security Bureau, hearing of this plan, sent word that any driver daring to take the sculpture would lose his license. The students then hired six of the familiar Beijing carts, which resemble a bicycle in the front and a flat cart with two wheels in the back. Four carts carried the sections of the statue, and two others hauled tools and materials. Students from the Central Academy, along with other students from the academies of crafts, drama, music, and dance, accompanied the carts to the square. The procession was led by a bearer of the Central Academy's flag, followed by two columns of strong young people, who guarded the carts that carried the statue. Other students marched along as an outer guard.

The route for transporting the statue to Tiananmen Square had been announced: a left turn outside the academy gate, then westward to the Donghua-men, the east gate of the Forbidden City, and along the road between the wall and the moat to the square. But this publicized route was issued to deceive the police, in case they were planning to stop us. In fact, the route turned right out of the academy, moved along Wangfujing, the well-known shopping street, then turned right along Changan Avenue past the Beijing Hotel.

The place on the square where the statue was to be erected had been chosen carefully. It was on the great axis, heavy with symbolism both cosmological and political, that extended from the main entrance of the Forbidden City, with the huge portrait of Mao Tse-tung (the leader of China who died in 1976) over it, to the Monument to the People's Heroes, which had become the command headquarters of the student movement. The statue was to be set up just across the broad avenue from the portrait of Mao, so that it would confront the Great Leader face to face.

When the procession arrived, about ten-thirty that night, a huge crowd, perhaps fifty thousand people, had gathered around the tall scaffolding of iron poles that had already been erected to support the statue. The parts were placed one on top of another and attached to this frame; plaster was poured into the hollow core, locking it onto a vertical iron pole, which extended from the ground up the center to hold the statue upright. The exposed iron supports were then cut away, leaving the statue freestanding. The base upon which it stood was also made of iron rods, about two meters in height, and later was covered with cloth. The Goddess of Democracy statue was designed so that, once assembled, it could not be taken apart again, but would have to be destroyed all at once.

The work continued through the night. A ring of students joined hands around the statue so that those working on it would be undisturbed. Only those involved in erecting the statue were allowed inside the circle.

By noon on May 30, the statue was ready for the unveiling ceremony. Journalists and others who were gathered there had become restless by midmorning and were showing signs of leaving. I warned the students of this and advised them to announce the time of the ceremony over the loudspeaker in order to persuade people to stay. The students said, "You speak English; why don't you make the announcement?" So I did, in my best English: "Ladies and gentlemen, please stay where you are. We will have the unveiling ceremony around twelve noon."

The ceremony was simple and very moving. A statement about the meaning of the statue had been prepared, written on a long banner stretched on poles near the figure. It was read over the loudspeaker by a woman, probably a student at the Broadcasting Academy, who had a good Mandarin accent. The statement was signed by the eight art academies that had sponsored the whole project: the four Central Academies—Fine Arts, Arts and Crafts, Drama, and Music; the Beijing Film Academy; the Beijing Dance Academy; the Academy of Chinese Local Stage Arts; and the Academy of Chinese Music. Like the sculpture itself, the statement was a piece of passionately dedicated improvisation; it was written on the banner in rather crude calligraphy. The statement was read:

Dear Compatriots and Fellow Students:

We, as proud citizens of China, have broken the autocracy of the government and now stand welcoming the Democracy Movement of 1989. All the people are of a single mind; to combat bravely the feudal autocracy. Fighting tirelessly through the days and nights of the past weeks, we have achieved victories one after another, because the people are invincible.

Now this autocratic government, possessing only animal characteristics, lacking all human feeling, has used the most shameless and scurrilous methods, violence and cheating, in their attempt to kill the Goddess of Democracy as a newborn infant in her cradle. But this coming of darkness proves only that they have reached the end of their road; the day of their doom has already arrived. They will be judged by all the people.

At this grim moment, what we need most is to remain calm and united in a single purpose. We need a powerful cementing force to strengthen our resolve: that is the Goddess of Democracy.

Democracy, how long it is since we last saw you . . .

You are the hope for which we thirst, we Chinese who have suffered decades of repression under the feudal autocracy!

You are the symbol of every student in the Square, of the hearts of millions of people!

You are the soul of the 1989 Democracy Movement!

You are the Chinese nation's hope for salvation!

Today, here in the People's Square, the people's goddess stands tall and announces to the whole world: A consciousness of democracy has awakened among the Chinese people! The new era has begun! From this piece of ancient earth grows the tree of democracy and freedom, putting forth gorgeous flowers and a bountiful harvest of fruit!

The statue of the Goddess of Democracy is made of plaster, and of course cannot stand here forever. But as the symbol of the people's hearts, she is divine and inviolate. Let those who would sully her beware: the people will not permit this!

We believe strongly that this darkness will pass, that the dawn must come. On the day when real democracy and freedom come to China, we must erect another Goddess of Democracy here in the Square, monumental, towering, and permanent. We have strong faith that that day will come at last. We have still another hope: Chinese people, arise! Erect the statue of the Goddess of Democracy in your millions of hearts!

Long live the people!

Long live freedom!

Long live democracy!

When the time came for the actual unveiling, two Beijing residents, a woman and a man, were chosen at random from the crowd and invited into the circle to pull the strings that would remove the pieces of red and blue cloth. As the veil fell, the crowd burst into cheers. There were shouts of "Long live democracy!" and other slogans, and some began to sing the Internationale. A musical performance was given by students from the Central Academy of Music: a choral rendition of the Hymn to Joy from Beethoven's Ninth Symphony, a Chinese song, and then the Internationale again. A planned performance by students from the Central Academy of Dance had to be canceled because of the pressure of the crowd and the lack of space.

I stood there with the huge crowd gazing up at this ten-meter-high work—the Goddess of Democracy. It was scarcely a masterpiece of world sculpture, made in three days and nights by a group of undergraduate students. And yet it was the greatest sculpture I had ever seen, and the ceremony had been the greatest I had ever attended.

After the unveiling ceremony we returned to the Central Academy. I invited all the young sculptors to lunch, but in the end they insisted on inviting me. The lunch was brief because the students badly needed to get some sleep. They had not slept for four days. I thought, These young people are the future of China; why can't Deng Xiaoping [the supreme leader in China] appreciate the youth of his own country!

During the early evening on that day there was a strong wind and rainstorm, and students rushed back to the square to see if the statue had been damaged. But it had endured this first serious test without harm. We took this as a good omen, but we were wrong.

On the terrible night of June 3 I was moving around the square for some forty hours without sleep. Afterward, I could no longer go on living at the Central Academy—it was too dangerous—and most of the students and faculty had fled when I returned there the day after the massacre. That was the last time during that period that I saw the students who made the statue. They were frightened, with good reason, and had dispersed to safer places. I interviewed several of them a year later in the summer of 1990. They were all safe.

The Goddess of Democracy stood in Tiananmen Square for five days. The toppling of the Goddess by the army, the final heartrending symbolic act, was witnessed by millions of television viewers. Pushed over by a tank, the Goddess fell forward and to the right, so that its arms and the torch struck the ground first, breaking off. The statue must have been quickly and easily reduced to rubble, mixing with all the other rubble in the square, to be cleared away by the army as part of its deceitful show of cleanliness and order.

The idea behind the statue could not be so easily destroyed, however. As the statement at the unveiling said, the statue that was built at that time was not designed to be permanent. It was intended, however, to endure as an image of the desire of the great mass of Chinese people to achieve the ideals it symbolized, the ideals of liberty and democracy.

CHINESE VIEWS OF LIBERTY, DEMOCRACY, AND
THE PURSUIT OF SCIENTIFIC KNOWLEDGE,
BY FANG LI ZHI

EDITOR: Professor Fang, the Statue of Liberty is a leading symbol in the world of human and political freedom. The statue is known in China, particularly among Chinese students. During the student-led demonstrations for democracy that took place in Beijing, in Tiananmen Square, in May and June 1989, a group of art students designed and constructed a statue closely resembling the Statue of Liberty. They called the statue the Goddess of Democracy. What is known in China about the Statue of Liberty, its origins, and its meaning? What was the connection between the statue in New York Harbor and the Goddess of Democracy that stood for five days in the Chinese capital?

DR. FANG: At the time of the pro-democracy movement and the demonstrations in Beijing and in other cities in China, in 1989, I was not able to view the Goddess of Democracy statue in Tiananmen Square. Government authorities, secret police, watched my movements very carefully. They accused me of fomenting the discord and the dissent against the government. I could not view directly the activities of the students or the statue. Of course, I learned about it from colleagues and friends. I learned also that it was destroyed by the authorities after a brief period. Many students and intellectuals in China know, of course, what the Statue of Liberty in New York represents.

EDITOR: Can you tell us about the democracy movement in the People's Republic of China?

DR. FANG: The pro-democracy demonstrations in Tiananmen Square in May and June of 1989 became news throughout the world. People everywhere were fascinated by it. Few people outside of China know or realize, however, that earlier in this century another pro-democracy movement took place in China, which exerted a significant influence on later thinking. In May 1919, after World War I, students and intellectuals gathered also in Tiananmen Square, in the center of Beijing, and demonstrated for democratic reforms. This gathering came to be known as the May Fourth Movement. In both periods, students from Beijing University played a leading role. Scientists, too, were involved in the pro-democracy demonstrations, both in 1919 and again in 1989.

There was one difference between the two events, however. Before and after World War I, a number of different areas in mainland China had become colonies of Western nations. Germany, for example, had a colony, not unlike the British colony at Hong Kong, situated at Shandong province. Russia also had a small colony in China. With Germany's defeat in World War I, it had to abandon its colony in China. But at the same time the Japanese government, a rising Asian power, was demanding the right to colonize a portion of China and putting a great deal of pressure on China.

The May Fourth Movement in 1919 crystallized opposition to the European colonization of China and the demands of the Japanese to colonize China. But this movement also was thoroughly democratic in nature. In 1919 and again in 1989, students, teachers, intellectuals, and others joined together to ask the government to make reforms along democratic lines.

EDITOR: What is the dominant idea of democracy among students and intellectuals in China? What kind of democracy do Chinese students want to see develop in China? Would this be a Western-style democracy, as exists in the United States and in Europe?

DR. FANG: In China there is a belief that the core concept of democracy is universal; it is not bound to a particular country, or people, or tradition. Just as the idea of science is universal, so too is the idea of democracy considered to be part of the aspiration and the desire of peoples everywhere. I would go further, to say that human freedom, liberty, human rights, are considered in China, as in the West, to be universal truths. All peoples by their nature, according to human nature, desire and deserve to live in freedom.

EDITOR: What are the dominant ideas of freedom in China, among Chinese students and intellectuals, for example?

111

DR. FANG: I believe the key point about freedom, or about democracy, is the idea of the guarantee of a right to have a free choice in the way one lives. This is a core concept. To have the right, and to be able to exercise the right, to freely choose what one wishes to say publicly, or what one wishes to study, or to read about.

Let me give you a good example. Early in the twentieth century Chinese women began to understand and to demand as a right that they should have the ability on their own to choose or find a husband to love and to live with. That too is part of the concept of free choice. The Chinese people today, as they did after World War I, think a great deal about freedom. They continue to desire freedom and to demand greater freedom than they have in reality. China today is, of course, ruled by a dictatorship. Yet the struggle for freedom continues, even though the pro-democracy movements in 1919 and again in 1989 were crushed by the government.

EDITOR: Can you tell us what the relationship is between the desire among Chinese students for freedom and democracy, on the one hand, and the desire for socialism, on the other?

DR. FANG: China, of course, today calls itself a socialist or, more accurately, a communist society. But there are many forms of socialism. The Chinese people, I feel safe to say, reject the violent and brutal form that was identified with Stalin and Stalinist rule in the Soviet Union. I believe students and intellectuals, for the most part, want to embrace a form of socialism that coexists with democracy, as is the case in certain Western European societies.

Many Chinese students are pro-socialist. They identify socialism with the concept of reducing or eliminating the gap that often exists between the rich and the poor, not only in China but in many societies.

EDITOR: What is the relationship in China between the ideas of democracy, human rights, and science? Is there a close link between science and democracy, from the Chinese viewpoint?

DR. FANG: It is not widely known, but in China, going back to the early part of this century, the ideas of democracy and of science were closely connected. A slogan of political reformers, early in the century, ran as follows: "We need to invite into China Mr. Democracy and Mr. Science, both together." The reformers who sought to make China more democratic also tried to make China more congenial to the sciences. The view was that without democracy, there could be no science, or at least no science that could claim to be science of the highest quality.

As I said earlier, Chinese scientists have long been in the forefront of movements to make China more democratic and more free. In the 1989 pro-democracy demonstrations, Chinese scientists, once again, were active.

If you think about it, the practice of science fundamentally depends on the ability to think freely. And the ability to think freely can arise only in a society that is democratic, that protects the rights of its citizens. This lies behind the close connection, in the Chinese view, between the two ideas.

EDITOR: Dr. Fang, can you give us some impressions of Chinese students and a comparison between students in China and students in the United States whom you have come to know?

DR. FANG: My observation in the limited time I have lived in the United States is that American students, for the most part, enjoy a way of life that is so much easier and more comfortable than the life that Chinese students experience. American students enjoy much freedom. The material level of life is much higher than in China.

On the other hand, students in China by and large live under the poorest of conditions. They do not enjoy the freedoms that American students enjoy. For example, every university in China has what amounts to a police station that watches over the activities of students. It is very difficult for students to express what is on their minds, certainly to do so openly. But there is one difference, in another respect. Most students in China are very involved in politics, at least in political ideas and longings, even if they have to be careful what they talk about in public and whom they talk with. Many students in China are very involved in the future of their country, the fate of their people, and think a lot about these questions. In the United States, however, my impression is that the majority of American students are not as politically or socially involved as Chinese students, even though they have every type of freedom and are able to get involved in public life.

EDITOR: Dr. Fang, do you have other thoughts to share about democracy?

DR. FANG: I want to conclude with my strong belief—and many of my former students and colleagues in China share this belief—that one of the great movements in world history at this time is the movement toward freedom and human rights. This is a universal movement. Freedom and human rights have become a major world trend and a world force.

I believe the recognition is growing among all peoples that freedom is part of their nature and their purpose in life. It is part of the birthright of every human being.

I am optimistic about the future of freedom and democracy in the world, and in my own country of China in particular. The struggle for freedom and democracy will continue. Today, the Communist system throughout the world is in serious decline. So too in China. I believe that communism eventually will come to an end in China, as it has in other parts of the world.

There will be progress and there also will be some backsliding. But, ultimately, I believe strongly that the Chinese people someday in the future will embrace freedom and be in a position to enjoy the rights that are associated with freedom and democracy.

The Engineering of Symbols
The Statue of Liberty and Other Nineteenth-Century Towers and Monuments

DAVID P. BILLINGTON

igantic symbols such as the Statue of Liberty carry both intended meanings and a significance unpredicted by their designers. The stronger the designers' vision, the more powerfully will the intended meaning dominate those unanticipated ideas that grow up after the symbol's completion. So strong was John Roebling's vision of the Brooklyn Bridge, like Gustave Eiffel's vision of his tower of three hundred meters, for example, that Roebling's ideas still dominate all discussions of that greatest of nineteenth-century bridges.

That force of vision, however, has not been operable in the case of the Statue of Liberty, which has come to symbolize things never imagined by its designer. One reason for this unforeseen turn of events is that the statue is really two separate buildings that are not integrated in any visual way. One is a self-supporting engineering structure designed by Gustave Eiffel, and the other is a totally invertebrate skin shaped by Frédéric-Auguste Bartholdi. The statue in its apparent solidity is the work of a sculptor, whereas the statue in its actual hollow lightness is the work of an engineer. Unlike similar monuments of its day, the statue embodies the notion grown powerful during the past two hundred years that appearance and utility are separate and unrelated features of building. Thus the symbol of the visible woman and the structure hidden within the hollow form represent two distinct and unrelated traditions: the sculptor's studio and the engineer's construction site.

I want here to describe that engineering tradition, focusing especially on Gustave Eiffel's contributions to it. A brief discussion of three other monuments of the 1880s that characterize that tradition at the end of the nineteenth century will illuminate the understanding of the Statue of Liberty from an engineering perspective.

THE MONUMENTAL EVENTS

Between the centennial celebrations of those two great eighteenth-century political revolutions of 1776 and 1789, there arose a series of monuments whose own centennials we have only recently celebrated. These four monuments—the Brooklyn Bridge (1883), the Statue of Liberty (1886), the Washington Monument (1888), and the Eiffel Tower (1889)—are still standing and still serving their original purposes. Although each was viewed a century ago as the culmination of a historical process stretching back to the eighteenth century, today we can recognize in these immense structures much more of the symbolism of the era from 1876 to 1889 than of the years from 1776 to 1789. They are the permanent, archeological records of the ideals of an age when the Western world entered the vast and portentous house of technology. Each monument stands for the ideals of engineering and of society. And for each of them our story begins in 1876.

PHILADELPHIA CENTENNIAL OF 1876

The Centennial Exposition, celebrating one hundred years of United States history, opened in Philadelphia on May 10, 1876, when President Ulysses S. Grant and Emperor Dom Pedro of Brazil turned on the 39-foot-high Corliss engine that both powered part of the fair and provided its most enduring symbol.[1] At the same time, in New York, John Roebling's 276-foot-high stone towers stood complete in the East River in preparation for the 1,595-foot span of the Brooklyn Bridge that would be started later on.[2]

Neither the stone bridge tower nor the metal steam engine served any direct commercial or social use in 1876. Both, however, stood for such future use in the most powerful possible ways. That is to say, they both stood as icons to the emergence of the United States as the world's most powerful nation.[3] They were both self-conscious monuments that, consistent with American pragmatism, were intended to be directly useful in the economy and to be symbols of national power and achievement.

These two objects of pure technology represented the most visually obvious of the two sides of modern technology: the structures and the machines—the fixed, permanent objects, on the one hand, and the moving, transient objects, on the other—that have completely reordered the world over the past two hundred years.

The bridge tower and the engine of 1876 stood at the dividing point in the development of those two centuries. George Corliss's engine is a straightforward enlargement of James Watt's 1787 steam engine; John Roebling's Brooklyn Bridge is a scaled-up version of Thomas Telford's 1826 Menai Straights Bridge. Each object of 1876 represented the culmination of a vast nineteenth-century reorientation of British and American society away from isolated rural communities and toward new networks focusing on industrialized and fast-growing cities. Therefore, each centennial monument stands for large-scale technology, which encouraged the building of high-density cities and, in turn, led aesthetically sensitive observers to contemplate the promise and the portent of a completely new type of civilization.

These two grand objects expressed better than anything else at the time the overlapping ideas of an emerging world, which would be based on scientific constructions, lead to a new social order, and provide a set of new forms with no visual precedent in the preindustrial world.

In short, the coming technological world would be scientific, it would radically alter society, and it would create totally new symbols. Above all, technology (which is used here to mean modern engineering) would give people control over their lives, both publicly as nations and privately as citizens. Public works, characterized by the bridge tower, would result in new cities; and private industry, represented by the engine, would usher in new freedom and prosperity.

We do not need to accept these overoptimistic views from 1876 uncritically to realize nevertheless that modern technology (and hence the modern world) cannot be understood without an analysis that explores its scientific and technological basis, its social context, and its symbolic power. Therefore, to understand such objects as the bridge and the engine, one must describe their workings first in scientific-technological terms, as measures of efficiency. For a physical structure, efficiency means the use of the least amount of material consistent with its required strength; for a machine, efficiency means the use of the least amount of energy consistent with its required power.

Efficiency as a scientific measure is, of course, only one aspect of technology, because savings in materials and energy must always be balanced by savings in cost and maintenance. These monetary measures are social, rather than scientific, calculations; they depend upon time and place, and they characterize the political and economic world in the same way that efficiency characterizes the physical and chemical world. The cost for a structure such as a bridge or other public works usually reflects political and social considerations; nothing reveals late-nineteenth-century urban politics more clearly than the fraudulent financing of the Brooklyn Bridge.[4] The cost of a machine, on the other hand, relates to private profit rather than public benefit. At the same time, just as public works need to be economical, so do the products of private industry need to benefit and not harm public life.

Ultimately, of course, technology must also be evaluated in terms that elude quantitative measurement but that account for those fundamental aspects of life that we describe by such words as *beautiful*, *ethical*, and *spiritual*. The Brooklyn Bridge is one of those objects of pure technology that has so impressed both the individual artist and the general public that it has become not only a social benefit to transportation but also an elegant park for the city resident, as well as an icon of even greater power than its cableless towers of 1876 revealed. For many artists, such as the poet Hart Crane and the painter Joseph Stella, the bridge became a spiritual event, a celebration of the human spirit comparable with the greatest works of art.[5] It is, in fact, now recognized to be a great work of art in its own right.

In the same way, the Corliss engine struck many leading artists of its day as a supreme aesthetic object that even inspired a spiritual awe and wonder.[6] Here again, we can find the marked difference between structures and machines: mass and energy, public benefit and private profit, and now a permanent symbol as opposed to a transient one. But the motion of the machine creates a different and more immediately striking response than the repose of the large-scale structure. The aesthetic of the machine, like that of the dance, the play, and the symphony, is transient but no less deep than that of a structure, the aesthetic of which is more like that of architecture, sculpture, painting, and photography.

The structure and the machine are built not to be isolated monuments but to be parts of large technological systems. The Brooklyn Bridge was intended as a primary link in the intraurban transportation networks of metropolitan New York; the Corliss engine formed the heart of the fully mechanized Centennial Exposition from which its power spread out through long rotating shafts. In its second life, that great engine powered the entire industrial community of Pullman, just south of Chicago. The bridge tower and the engine became, by 1883, the centerpieces of the most striking urban experiments in the United States: the connection between the largest and the third-largest cities, New York and Brooklyn— then an independent city—and the industrial might of America's soon-to-be-second-largest city, Chicago.[7]

These two objects, therefore, serve within two sorts of systems: the transportation network and the industrial process. The network is a static system, comparable to the static structures that help form it. The process is a dynamic system, comparable to the dynamic machines that help power it. In Pullman, Illinois, the Corliss engine provided power to convert raw materials and prefabricated parts into a finished railroad car, whereas in New York, the Brooklyn Bridge provided the means for carriages and tramways to carry people and goods, essentially unchanged, from one part of the city to another.

Soon the engine would be used as the center of a new network carrying electric power throughout the city just as other bridges, since 1830, already had helped to form a network of railroads connecting cities together. Similarly, steam engines had already entered the factory to produce chemical products as well as to power mechanical assemblies. In a general way, therefore, we can characterize modern engineering from the centennial times onward as composed of objects and systems, each of which has two complementary types: structures and machines are the objects, which correspond roughly to networks and processes, which are the systems.

THE CELEBRATION OF 1883

Seven years after the centennial, both icons were in full service, the bridge open to traffic and the engine powering Pullman's model town in Illinois. At the same time the bridge tower had now a rival in Chicago, where the first modern skyscraper had appeared in 1879; in that same year also, in New Jersey, Edison had designed his successful light bulb, which in 1882 allowed him to build the world's first central power station for generating electricity from steam engine power. The opening of the Brooklyn Bridge on May 24, 1883, thus characterized not only a highly visual and restructured world but also one that would become mechanized by the unseen power of electricity. Symbols like the Brooklyn Bridge, being technological, thereby stood for both a visible change and an unseen new power in society. Technology from now on would be both a form and a force; it would be of obvious and immediate benefit and also hold unclear and long-term potential.

There would be a new dimension of technology, only partly understood, to go along with the older and more easily grasped meaning of technology as form and structure. The attempt to understand persists today and is no more resolved than when sensitive observers first felt those unresolved tensions within nineteenth-century technology. The American chronicler Henry Adams, for example, felt he understood engineering forms and structures, such as cathedrals, in a visual sense, but he had difficulty understanding the power plant or an engine as a visual form. Adams referred metaphorically to the former as "the Virgin" and to the latter as "the Dynamo." This struggle for clarity expresses itself in the great monuments that appeared in the 1880s. In the four solutions devised in those monuments we can see what resolutions of the problem seemed possible both then and now.

THE WASHINGTON MONUMENT AND THE EIFFEL TOWER

In the Washington Monument, form is entirely historical and imitative; the originality lies in the immense scale and the location in a city lacking in history. It is pure technology in a material and a form carried over from the ancient world. For the monument, the year 1876 marked a time of new beginning, when the Corps of Engineers took over its design and construction after a stub column had stood unfinished for two decades. A cutaway diagram of the obelisk would show clearly the amateurish heavy base walls, surmounted by the thin masonry structure designed after 1876 by the Corps.

There also appeared at this time plans for a tower of 1,000 feet in height, proposed by engineers in Philadelphia for the centennial. This conical form, similar to the one proposed by Richard Trevithick forty years earlier for London, provides a context for Eiffel's far greater work. It was Eiffel alone who saw the tower in terms of a radically new form—a solution to the engineering problem of wind force that was central to nineteenth-century railroad building.

The Eiffel Tower exemplifies a structure designed to control wind force by means of its form rather than its mass. The Washington Monument, on the other hand, controls wind force by its mass and is therefore a nearly pure example of how a form controls gravity loads. Both the Eiffel Tower (1889) and the Washington Monument (1888) commemorate in prominent capital structures the great revolutions of the eighteenth century: the one that in 1789 ended the traditional order of old Europe; the other that in 1776 began the new democratic-technological civilization in which we now live. Until the twentieth century, these were the two tallest works of man, and each has to this day visually dominated the capital of its nation.

The obelisklike Washington Monument is still the highest masonry structure ever built. The marble and granite carry all the vertical dead load and the horizontal wind load. The structure is a slightly tapered vertical straight line. Its primary scientific function is to carry itself by compression between layers of stone. Since the stones cannot carry tension between their joints, the tendency to overturn under wind load must be counteracted by the dead weight alone.

Thus the tower gets thicker as it approaches the base, where the wind-overturning effect is greatest and at the same time the dead load will also be correspondingly the greatest. The base is 55 feet, 1.5 inches square, with 15-foot-thick walls, while the top of the 500-foot shaft is 34 feet, 5.5 inches square, with 18-inch-thick walls.

This solidity, representing resistance to load, creates a naturally closed form that limits its direct use by visitors to the view from the very top, where a small number of sealed-in people can get a fine look at Washington, D.C. Only a few can be at the top at once (the elevator holds thirty people) as there is little room (well under 1,000 square feet) and no facilities for anything other than looking out the eight windows, which provide a total of about 33 square feet of glass.

The closed masonry column of the Washington Monument clearly stands as a dominant element in the carefully laid-out immensity of formal Washington's landscape. Its form provides all visitors to the capital with a striking distant vista of what might be called an immense structure in a broad park.

The Eiffel Tower, by contrast, might be called a vast technological park set in a high structure. Indeed, the Washington Monument's principal use is as a decoration to be admired from afar; almost the only people who seem to approach it closely come to stand in line for the short trip to the top, as there is almost no intention for it to be a part of any plan to make use of the immediately surrounding lawns.

The monument, scientifically speaking, is an efficient masonry column; from a sociological perspective, it is a closed trip to view the city from above; symbolically, it is an elegant example of pure form that serves to orient every sightseer from a distance. By contrast, the Eiffel Tower is an efficient metal cantilever, a popular open trip in a park overlooking the city, and an elegant example of pure form that engages every visitor not just from a distance but also from the intimate perspective of ascent and leisurely wandering through its open structure.

That Eiffel could create this unique and enduring monument is a result of his engineering experience in the design and construction of large-scale bridges elevated across valleys on slender shaped towers. Moreover, he thought of these works in terms of three basics of structural engineering: as efficient forms, as competitive construction, and as elegant additions to the landscape. It was this unity of thought that raised Eiffel's structures to the level of art and made

Fig. 8.1. The Rouzat Viaduct over the Sioule River near Gannat, France. Built in 1869 by Gustave Eiffel, the Rouzat carries a single-track rail line. Two 59-meter-high wrought iron towers support three 60-meter trellis girder spans. The towers, curving outward at the base to reduce the forces from wind loading, show the beginning of Eiffel's design style, which culminated in the Eiffel Tower twenty years later. Source: Collection of David P. Billington.

him one of the three greatest structural artists of the nineteenth century (along with Thomas Telford and John Roebling). A brief review of Eiffel's career in bridge design leading up to his towers of the 1880s, the hidden one in the Statue of Liberty and the exposed one on the Champs de Mars, will give some idea of his art.

THE TOWERS OF EIFFEL

Between 1867 and 1869, Eiffel constructed in France four viaducts along the rail line between Gannat and Commentry in the Massif Central west of Vichy. Of the four, the viaduct at Rouzat (fig. 8.1) is visually the most striking and accessible, since the highway passes directly under the viaduct as it crosses the Sioule River.[8] In this viaduct, for the first time, Eiffel used iron towers to reflect visually the influence of the lateral wind loads, spreading the towers out in a curve to meet the masonry foundations.

In 1875, the Royal Portuguese Railway opened an international competition for the construction of a bridge over the Douro River near Oporto, Portugal. The eight different designs submitted with builders' fixed prices summarize the ideas for long-span bridges that had been developed up to that time.[9] The two simplest forms were

Fig. 8.2. Pia Maria Bridge over the Douro River, Oporto, Portugal. Completed in 1877 by Gustave Eiffel, this 160-meter span is a wrought iron crescent-shaped arch rising 42.5 meters at its crown. Eiffel's bid with this design was the lowest in an international design construction competition. Reprinted by permission of Centre Georges Pompidou, Paris.

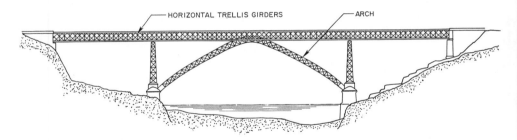

Fig. 8.3. An alternative design entered in the international design competition for the Pia Maria Bridge. The heavy horizontal trellis girders and gabled arch here provide support only at the midspan. Drawing by T. Agans, Princeton University, Princeton, New Jersey. Source: Collection of David P. Billington.

priced the lowest; one of these was Eiffel's new crescent arch, undeniably the more elegant of the two and also a full 31 percent less expensive than the next-cheapest design (figs. 8.2 and 8.3). The Douro competition confirmed Eiffel, at the age of 43, as the leading bridge designer in Europe. It also showed that the more beautiful form can coincide with the most useful structure—that is, the required utility with the least cost. In fact, Eiffel's design has also provided to be durable: the bridge stands today in fine condition after more than a century of continuous use.

The wide lateral spreading of Eiffel's arches in the Douro Bridge (also known as the Pia Maria Bridge) not only gives greater lateral stiffness than the competing designs do but also makes the crescent form visually more striking. The crescent becomes narrower but deeper as it rises from the hinges. Such an idea is highly rational, but it is unique to Eiffel. It is a mark of his style to give three-dimensional variation to structures with an overall form that is largely two-dimensional. The Douro Bridge is handsome in pure profile (its two-dimensional aspect), but in addition it provides visual surprise and delight from different perspectives (its three-dimensional aspect). Eiffel had sought a form that would be both the most graceful and the best able to carry the bridge's load. Moreover, using the crescent form with hinges at the supports markedly simplified the necessary calculations.

When, in 1879, Eiffel received the contract for an even larger bridge at Garabit in the Massif Central near St. Flour (fig. 8.4), he modified his crescent form to produce a higher arch.[10] The most obvious difference between the Douro and the Garabit bridges lies in the center of the span: whereas in the former, the horizontal trellis girder is interrupted by the arch, in the latter, that girder is visually continuous and structurally distinct. In part, the difference arises because at Garabit the railway is much higher above the valley than it is at Douro. The flatter Douro form leads to higher forces, and dropping the arch fully below the railway as at Garabit would have increased the forces noticeably. Nevertheless, the Douro form is less satisfactory because it superimposes the arch on the girders without integrating the two visually. Any increase in costs at Douro for an even flatter arch would have had no effect on the outcome of the competition. The Douro Bridge was the best example of structural art in iron arch bridges built up to 1877; the bridge at Garabit is the greatest work of structural art—that is, the most efficient, economical, and handsome—ever built in iron arch form and the masterpiece of Eiffel's bridge career.

Therefore, by 1884 Eiffel had become the leading engineer working with iron structures. To get a sense of his greatness as a structural artist, we can compare his Garabit Viaduct with the equally large Müngstner Bridge, designed by Anton Rieppel and built over the Wuppertal in Germany (fig. 8.5).[11] Like Eiffel's de-

Fig. 8.4. The Garabit Viaduct over the Truyère River near Saint Flour, France, by Gustave Eiffel. This 165-meter span was the longest in the world when completed in 1884. The two-hinged arch is separated visually from the thin horizontal girder, resulting in an appearance different from that of the Pia Maria Bridge over the Douro River. Reprinted by permission of Department of Art and Archeology, Princeton University, Princeton, New Jersey.

sign, the German bridge was economical and efficient, but unlike the Garabit, it is not a visual masterpiece. I shall characterize the visual difference by two examples: the short verticals between arch and deck and the long vertical structure from the deck down to the base of the arches.

In the Müngstner the short verticals are thin in profile compared to the great width of the long verticals. In the Garabit these two sets of verticals are similarly shaped; the result has a unity that is lacking in the Müngstner. The long verticals in Garabit are clearly separated from the arch and hence articulated as freestanding towers, whereas the Müngstner's long verticals go into the arch trusswork and create a visual confusion of form. The consequence of these visual differences is that the Garabit has stimulated artists of the first rank, whereas, to my knowledge, the Müngstner bridge has never entered the art world as an aesthetic object of high merit. For example, Le Corbusier in his most famous book, *Towards a New Architecture*,[12] begins "The Engineer's Aesthetic" chapter with a photograph of the Garabit; that bridge also provided Sigfried

Fig. 8.5. The Müngstner Bridge (Müngstnerbrücke) in Wuppertal, Germany. Built in 1897 by Anton Rieppel, this fixed steel arch with a 170-meter span is penetrated at the ends by wide vertical truss structures. From *Aesthetik im Brückenbau* (Leipzig and Vienna, 1928). Source: Collection of F. Hartmann.

Giedion with a powerful theme for his influential work *Space, Time, and Architecture*.[13] In the end, it is Eiffel as engineering artist who makes the difference, and like Telford and Roebling, Eiffel combined aesthetic motives with the highest technical discipline and talent. It was not aesthetics as opposed to or at the expense of efficiency or economy. It is ironic, therefore, that Eiffel's only structure in the United States is totally hidden and was, moreover, not even correctly built.

THE STATUE OF LIBERTY: COLOSSUS DISARMED

In 1876 the Brooklyn Bridge was not New York's only unfinished monument. At the Philadelphia centennial and later on in New York City's Herald Square stood the solitary torch-bearing arm of the Statue of Liberty. Not only was there by 1876 insufficient money to build the body of the statue but also there was quite literally no engineering plan for it. Bartholdi had at first employed as his engineer Eugène Emmanuel Viollet-le-Duc, architectural theorist and principal designer for the restoration of the French Gothic cathe-

127

Fig. 8.6. Interior view of the Statue of Liberty. The central iron pylon made up of four cross-braced columns and a secondary framework of flat iron armature bars connecting the ribs of the exterior copper skin to the iron skeleton permit the copper skin to flex as it responds to wind, heat, and cold. Reprinted by permission of National Park Service, Statue of Liberty National Monument.

drals. Viollet's ideas for the structure were mercifully discarded after his death in 1879, and Eiffel came upon the scene to make a straightforward tower design of no inherent aesthetic interest. Because it was to be totally concealed, the statue design did not touch his visual imagination; the result therefore is a good engineering application of efficiency and economy, but one without elegance (fig. 8.6).

One consequence of concealing the structure is that structural defects do not become readily visible and consequently can lead to increased difficulties. In fact, a severe defect was built into the arm of the statue because the firm of Gaget, Gauthier, and Company changed Eiffel's straightforward design (fig. 8.7), displacing the arm by about two feet and connecting it to the main pylon improperly (fig. 8.8). The outside arm element was then ended in the middle of another member rather than at the intersection of members (point A in fig. 8.8).[14] Such poor construction forced the closing of public

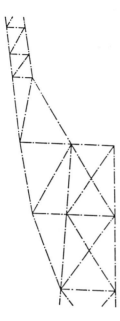

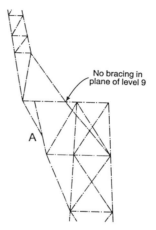

Fig. 8.7. Eiffel's original design for the arm structure of the Statue of Liberty, c. 1880. From *Civil Engineering* 55 (1): 35. Source: Collection of David P. Billington.

Fig. 8.8. Arm structure of the Statue of Liberty as built in 1885 by Gaget, Gauthier, and Company. At point A the design incorporates a faulty connection. From *Civil Engineering* 55. Source: Collection of David P. Billington.

access to the arm and torch early in this century and in the restoration necessitated a costly repair. It is one aspect of engineering as an art form that the full exposure and expression of structure can lead to works not only of great beauty but also of efficiency, economy, and ease of inspection and maintenance.

It is useful in this context to illustrate the deep cultural confusion over the engineer as artist by quoting from Marvin Trachtenberg's otherwise excellent 1976 study, *The Statue of Liberty*. Trachtenberg quotes Eiffel's defense of his tower and states that Eiffel's "intoxication led him on to an outburst defending himself from the (justifiably violent) protest of the cultural establishment against the Tower's abuse of the old scale of the city."[15] Trachtenberg thus appears to approve of the violent protest from those who preferred to see the tower unbuilt, and, moreover, he puts down Eiffel's defense not only as an "outburst" but as like "a typical engineer, Eiffel manifests a total insensitivity—like the modern highway builder—to the effect of his construction on the traditional fabric of human life."

Such an outburst, in an otherwise scholarly and well-written book, betrays two deep cultural confusions that need to be dispelled for a proper interpretation of the monuments of the 1880s and a recognition of the building issues of the 1980s and the 1990s. The first confusion relates to the engineer as artist. Trachtenberg says earlier, "That the aesthetic of the future should have been affected by the works of Eiffel—particularly his tower—is curious, because it was so unintentional. Eiffel's conscious taste was very conventional not only in the 'architecture' with which he clothed his pristine engineering, but in the pompous furnishings he surrounded himself with (even in his 'laboratory' atop the tower)."[16] This densely packed reservoir of misunderstanding assumes that Eiffel's aesthetic was unintentional, that his taste was conventional, that he willingly clothed his structures in fake facades, and that the proof of his conventional taste lies in his choice of furniture.

That Eiffel's aesthetic was mature and well in advance of his Parisian critics of the 1880s I have argued at length elsewhere and will not repeat here except to stress his central role in the new tradition that has flowered in the twentieth century with such structural artists as Robert Maillart, Pierluigi Nervi, Christian Menn, and Heinz Isler.[17] To state that Eiffel's taste was conventional betrays a confusion between design for the public and design for oneself. Structural artists focus their aesthetic intentions on public works and on the free play of forms within the disciplines of efficiency and economy. Such a vision cannot carry over to clothing and furniture. Perhaps the Romantic movement made it seem essential to art that the avant-garde artist dress and live in an "artistic" fashion. It is no secret that some artists can be comfortable in so-called conventional surroundings, and it is quite true, as Trachtenberg stresses, that engineers as a group appear to be quite conventional in such things. But in their own art, such people, at their best, are so thoroughly unconventional as to shock the sensitivities of those who reveled in the heavy stone facades of the distant past.

Eiffel did not clothe his pristine structures with ornament. All of his major bridges remain free from the conventional dressings forced on most nineteenth-century designers by stone-faced aesthetes. His 1884 design for the Eiffel Tower shows the pure structure; the accretions to it were not part of Eiffel's concept. He did not refer to them in his defense of the tower or in his later writings on it.

The second deep cultural confusion in the discussion of Eiffel lies in the assertion that he, "as a typical engineer, manifests a total insensitivity—like the modern highway builder—to the effect of his construction on the traditional fabric of human life." Here Trachtenberg casts engineers both then and now as careless destroyers of a humane landscape. Eiffel was well aware of the dramatic effect that his tower and other works had on their surroundings, and he believed that effect to be good. He was sensitive to it but approvingly so. A more cogent case can be made for the assertion that those opposed to the tower were insensitive to the possibilities for new forms to improve the fabric of urban life. Like Jean Louis Charles Garnier, designer of the heavy stone Paris Opera, they clung to the fading ideal of stone or stonelike facades as the only appropriate art of city building.

Trachtenberg's aesthetic sensitivity is, in fact, too good to avoid the simple conclusion that Eiffel's art was the greatest of his time. After complaining about engineers, he gives this summary of Eiffel's pure engineering works: "The resultant purity and harmony of forms of visionary scale, such as in the Garabit bridge or the piers of the tower, approach true sublimity."[18] Of course some engineers are insensitive, as are some architects and some political leaders. But the great engineers, from Telford through Eiffel to Maillart, Menn, and Isler, are deeply sensitive to the effects that their works produce. Like Fazlur Khan, designer of the Chicago Hancock Tower, which itself has received praise and condemnation just as the Eiffel Tower did, the best engineers have sought to create new and handsome forms to enrich urban life.

This discussion brings us back to the Statue of Liberty and helps to explain why it was of little abiding interest for Gustave Eiffel. In his writings he continually referred to the Douro and Garabit bridges, to several other bridges, and to the Eiffel Tower in Paris. But only rarely did he refer to the Statue of Liberty. When he did mention the statue, it was mainly to be sure that it was not attributed completely to Bartholdi. He kept no account or souvenir of it.[19] His lack of interest stemmed from the invisibility of his structure; it thus did not stimulate his artistic imagination.

The statue, though, is a significant engineering work because of what it does not show. It is characteristic of one view of engineering—i.e., as the hidden, nonaesthetic servant of the vision belonging to other professions. Such was not the defining vision of Eiffel or of the other engineering artists of the past two hundred years, but it is consistent with views held by many others about engineers and engineering. Although the Statue of Liberty may not reveal the potential for new forms, it does at least raise the issue of appropriate monuments, which is today still of signal importance.

NOTES

1. Phillip T. Sandhurst, *The Great Centennial Exhibition, Critically Described and Illustrated by Phillip T. Sandhurst and Others* (Philadelphia: P. W. Ziegler and Company, 1876), 361–69.

2. Mary C. Black, *Old New York in Early Photographs: 1853–1901* (New York: New York Historical Society and Dover Publishers, 1973), vi–x.

3. Dian O. Belanger, "The Corliss at Pullman," *Technology and Culture* 25, no. 1 (January 1984): 83–90.

4. David G. McCullough, *The Great Bridge* (New York: Simon and Schuster, 1972).

5. Alan Trachtenberg, *Brooklyn Bridge: Fact and Symbol* (New York: Oxford University Press, 1965).

6. Belanger, "Corliss," 85.

7. Stanley Buder, *Pullman: An Experiment in Industrial Order and Community Planning, 1880–1930* (New York: Oxford University Press, 1967).

8. I. Insolera, "I grandi viadotti di Eiffel nel Massif Central," *Zodiac* 13 (1964): 61–111; W. Neumann, "Le centenaire des premiers viaducs d'Eiffel," *La Via du Rail*, no. 1211 (1969): 10–14, 39–41.

9. T. Seyrig, "Le pont sur le Douro," *Memoires des Travaux de la Société des Ingénieurs Civils* (September–October 1978): 734–816.

10. E. Deydier, *Le Viaduc de Garabit* (Paris: Editions Gerbert, 1960); Gustave Eiffel, *Notice sur le Viaduc de Garabit* (Paris: P. Dupont, 1888).

11. Friedrich Hartmann, *Asthetik im Brukenbau* (Vienna, 1928), 36–38.

12. Le Corbusier, *Towards a New Architecture*, trans. F. Etchells (London: Architectural Press, 1927).

13. Sigfried Giedion, *Space, Time, and Architecture: The Growth of a New Tradition*, 5th ed. rev. and enlarged (Cambridge, Mass.: Harvard University Press, 1967).

14. Rita Robison, "Saving the Lady," *Civil Engineering* (January 1985): 30–39.

15. Marvin Trachtenberg, *The Statue of Liberty* (New York: Viking, 1976), 148–49.

16. Ibid., 129–30.

17. David P. Billington, *The Tower and the Bridge: The New Art of Structural Engineering* (New York: Basic Books, 1983; paperback ed. Princeton, N.J.: Princeton University Press, 1985).

18. Trachtenberg, *Statue of Liberty*, 130.

19. Henri Loyrette, *Gustave Eiffel* (New York: Rizzoli, 1985), 100.

The Ultimate Gift

WILTON S. DILLON

Everything is stuff to be given away and repaid.

— MARCEL MAUSS

In Western civilization, perhaps the worst-case scenario of one group's presenting a monumental gift to another involved the legendary Trojan horse.[1] A Trojan prince, Paris, fell in love with Helen, the beautiful wife of the king of Sparta. Helen fled, or was forced to flee, to Troy. The Greeks swore vengeance on Paris and on Troy. For ten years, they laid siege to Troy but could not take the city. They built a huge wooden horse. Greek soldiers hid in the horse while the rest of the Greeks pretended to sail away. The curious Trojans dragged the horse inside the city walls, despite a priest's warning "I fear the Greeks, even when bringing gifts." That night, the Greek soldiers crept out of the horse, opened the city gates, and let in their compatriots to loot and burn the Asia Minor city. The legends outlive the archaeological evidence (fig. 9.1).

In striking contrast, during the presidency of Grover Cleveland (1885–89), the French left outside the "gates" of New York a gift of even more monumental proportions. Instead of soldiers inside, the

Fig. 9.1. *The Building of the Trojan Horse.* This famous painting by Venetian artist
Giovanni Domenico Tiepolo recounts the legend of the Trojan War (c. 1260 B.C.).
After failing to penetrate the walled city of Troy, the Greeks built a wooden horse,
concealed Greek soldiers in its hollow interior, and left it outside the city gates.
The Trojans brought the horse inside, and at night the Greek soldiers, along with
compatriots from ships offshore, burned Troy. Reprinted by permission of
Wadsworth Atheneum, Hartford, Connecticut, and Ella Gallup Sumner and Mary
Catlin Sumner Collection.

French brought a skeleton for Miss Liberty that represented the
state of the art of French civil engineering: Gustave Eiffel's iron
frame, influenced by his earlier designs for bridges. The outside
skin revealed breathtaking beauty, as art and engineering became
one. The curious New Yorkers did not drag the statue into Manhattan, though she had stood earlier in the streets of Paris, as shown in
the famous Victor Dargaud painting of 1883 (fig. 9.2).

The long buildup in France in preparing for the offering of the
gift had made Miss Liberty a part of the French national consciousness. Though motivated by enlightened self-interest—to find allies
in the preservation of republican government in France—the
French donors found their countrymen attaching great value to the
gift as the symbolic rays of light found their way into French popular culture, much as the statue would do for generations after her
arrival in the United States. James Tissot's painting *Ces Dames des
chars* reveals the delight that French circus fans took in Liberty's image (fig. 9.3).

Fig. 9.2. *La Statue de la Liberté de New York dans l'atelier du fondeur Bayet, rue de Chazelles.* This 1883 painting by Victor Dargaud shows Liberty and scaffolding outside the workshop of Gaget, Gauthier, and Company, where it was built. The statue, shortly before it was dismantled for shipment to New York, dominated the skyline of this Paris neighborhood. Photograph by M. L. Berthier. Reprinted by permission of Musée Carnavalet, Paris.

Fig. 9.3. *Ces Dames des chars* (The Ladies of the Circus). Executed in 1883–85, when the work on the Statue of Liberty was completed, James Tissot's painting depicts a scene from a French circus, illustrating the almost immediate popularization and appeal of Liberty's image. Source: Museum of Art, Rhode Island School of Design. Gift of Walter Lowry. Photograph by Cathy Carver. Reprinted by permission of Rhode Island School of Design.

The French ship of war *Isere* transported the statue to New York. Miss Liberty traveled the ocean in two hundred separate crates. The unveiling of the completed Statue of Liberty prompted a spectacular demonstration and parade on Liberty Day, October 28, 1886, with soldiers, sailors, and civilians marching on lower Broadway while Navy ships formed a flotilla in the harbor. Millions of visitors have since become pilgrims to the island to admire and climb inside one of the wonders of the world.

The Statue of Liberty remains the ultimate gift of one nation to another. Of all the gifts that have come to us, we may never have anything to compare with a gift of such scale, tangibility, and symbolism as the Statue of Liberty. What other nation has given a major national symbol to another and thus contributed to the identity and self-esteem of both?

French anthropology has focused on females as commodities of exchange or as targets of seizure in tribal warfare, leading to a lot of pushing and shoving to get the females home again. Coming from a civilization that prizes women, ranging from adoration of the Virgin Mary to Jeanne d'Arc and the ladies in Renoir's paintings, the Statue of Liberty gains new meaning in light of the feminist movement. Can our symbol inspire the liberation of women from household drudgery and the achievement of equal opportunity in the workplace? Liberty was not captured by a warring tribe and taken forever from her kith and kin, like the white woman in *Dances with Wolves*. She was offered to us in peace, purely as a gift. She has become a part of our psyche and ethos, a vital party to the delicate balancing act between feminine, masculine, and androgynous elements in our own cultures, and we are not about to let her go. She serves as a daily reminder that we live on a very small planet and that our motives to get along with each other are stronger when bonded by a beautiful piece of sculpture than by military force.

One of the universal maxims of gift giving and receiving is that both parties should attach value to the gift. We Americans have so internalized and appropriated the gift of Liberty as our own self-image, according her a stature shared only by Uncle Sam and the bald eagle, that we have almost forgotten where the gift of Miss Liberty came from. Victor Turner, in his *Forest of Symbols*, observes that "the significant elements of a symbol's meaning are related to what it does and what is done to it by and for whom."[2]

SHIFTING SYMBOLISM

Liberty Enlightening the World, as the Statue of Liberty was named by its creator, Frédéric-Auguste Bartholdi, stands in voluptuous contrast to the bald eagle, an earlier and concurrent American symbol. Indeed, there is a majesty in both symbols, and both have roots deep in classical antiquity. Roman warriors used a golden figure of an eagle as a sign of strength and bravery. Russian and Austrian emperors also had their eagles. Although the United States was anti-imperial at birth, the bald eagle was chosen as the national bird in 1782. For all the years between 1795 and 1933 we minted a $10 gold coin that showed an eagle clutching a laurel wreath. The eagle, however, has been eclipsed symbolically by the Statue of Liberty. While the bird itself continues to receive well-deserved attention from preservationists to prevent extinction, much psychocultural analysis remains to be done on the comparative strength of Uncle Sam, the bewhiskered male figure best known for recruiting in the military.

New Yorker cartoonist Peter Steiner told me that he found Liberty and Uncle Sam so different, appealing to different parts of a citizen's psyche, that he could not imagine putting them in the same frame. However, another *New Yorker* artist, Mischa Richter, has recently domesticated the two. One cartoon, of February 23, 1992, shows Liberty reclining in one lounge chair and Uncle Sam snoozing in another, with a tea table between them. In the caption Liberty is saying, "We have no friends, just allies." A sequel, on March 23, 1992, shows an upright Uncle Sam opening a refrigerator in the kitchen. On its doors are mottoes like "The only thing we have to fear is fear itself," "Give me liberty or give me death," and "A house divided against itself cannot stand." Liberty, reading a newspaper in the background, holds high her cup of coffee. A third cartoon, on April 27, 1992, in what now seems a genre, shows Liberty lounging with a newspaper, crown spikes aloft, feet on a footstool, listening to Uncle Sam, who is sitting in a neighboring chair and holding a cup of coffee, confess, "I have something to get off my chest—I don't know the words to the second verse of 'The Star-Spangled Banner'!"

The two images already had been joined in cartoons in the late nineteenth century, first showing Uncle Sam delivering money to Liberty for her pedestal (fig. 9.4) and later depicting Uncle Sam standing at the foot of Liberty to welcome immigrants to Ellis Island. A further examination of our own culture will clarify how this extraordinary symbol with roots in the ancient past became part of our pantheon of "American" symbols (which also includes Coca-Cola and blue jeans).

Fig. 9.4. "Uncle Sam Congrat-
ulates Miss Liberty." This cartoon by McDougal, from the
New York World, May 16, 1885,
shows Uncle Sam handing a
$50,000 check to Miss Liberty,
to be used for the statue's
pedestal. The cartoon honors
the citizens and workers who
contributed to the pedestal
fund. The *World's* publisher,
Joseph Pulitzer, himself an
immigrant, came to Liberty's
rescue with appeals to the public, and the pedestal was completed in May 1886. Reprinted
by permission of National Park
Service, Statue of Liberty
National Monument.

THE 1986 RITE OF PASSAGE

Awash in all kinds of symbols, the beautifully restored gift statue at
the celebrations on Independence Day, July 4, 1986, was surrounded below by officials and citizens and ships floating at her feet and
above by dirigibles and jets flying over in formation. Her hundredth
birthday brought President François Mitterrand, chief of the donor
state, which evolved out of ancient kingdoms and remnants of the
Roman Empire, to meet with President Ronald Reagan. As the head
of another of the world's great republics, Reagan symbolized the
continuing experiment with democracy and the shared philosophical antecedents from Greece and, later, the Enlightenment period
in France.

The philosophical dimensions of the occasion were eclipsed by
a stately procession of tall ships, a replay of the July 4, 1976,
pageantry marking the bicentennial of the Declaration of Independence (fig. 9.5). The French president's visit was scarcely noticed by
the *New York Times*. Perhaps Liberty had become so "American-

ized," so domesticated,[3] that it was hard to remember who gave her and how she got here. President and Madame Mitterrand did appear, however, at a spectacular pageant on Governor's Island, and they dined with the Reagans and members of the Cabinet.

A FRENCH ANTHROPOLOGIST LOOKS AT GIFTS

The gift of the statue needs to be understood in the context of more than two hundred years of reciprocity between France and the United States. Marcel Mauss (1872–1950), a famous French anthropologist and linguist, provides a framework for understanding such exchanges in his classic 1924 "Essai sur le don," translated into English as *The Gift*.[4] It draws on his studies of ancient civilizations, including Israel, Greece, Rome, Scandinavia, India, and China, as well as contemporary preliterate societies. From the study of all these groups, Mauss generalized three universal types of human obligations: the obligation to give, the obligation to receive, and the obligation to repay. These are fundamental and highly developed characteristics of most cultures, but they have particular significance in French civilization.

In my fieldwork in France, I found strong evidence of reciprocal ties between parents and children, friends and lovers, and families. These patterns extended to the workplace and, beyond that, to the nation.[5] A clear sense of history, in addition, helps French citizens remember what their nation has given, received, and repaid, whether the nation is governed through monarchial or republican forms. We Americans seem to lack a similar social inventory of gift bookkeeping. Our relatively short history, even ahistoricity, may explain why some of our rhythms of exchange are irregular or asymmetrical.

Extrapolating from Mauss's theories of reciprocity, I hope that future historians of United States–French relationships will rethink and reinterpret our interdependent histories through the lens of a gift-exchange metaphor. In the meantime, with Miss Liberty much in mind, I suggest we need to start with a look at the triangular relationships among Britain, France, and America. Reality would be ignored if relationships among the three were studied bilaterally.

For whatever the motives (the centuries-old rivalry between France and Britain, as manifest in Shakespeare's *Henry V*?), I think

Fig. 9.5. Independence Day celebration, New York Harbor, July 4, 1986. The Argentine frigate *Levatard* joins many other vessels to honor the nearly one hundred years of the Statue of Liberty's existence. Photograph by Jeff Tinsley. Reprinted by permission of Smithsonian Printing and Photographic Services, Smithsonian Institution, Washington, D.C.

the first great gift the French ever presented to the United States was a recognition of the country's right to exist—still a live issue in the world, one that haunts today's Arab-Israeli rivalry in the Middle East and fuels the tensions over the creation of a Palestinian state.

THE GIFT OF YORKTOWN

The first act—from our first ally—of recognition of our national independence from Great Britain came from France. The fact that France at the time was at war with Britain and that the American rebels were being freed from British masters meant that this validation was a by-product of the Anglo-French war. It nevertheless provided us with a practical basis on which our sovereign existence and separate identity depended. I refer, of course, to the great military triumph at the Battle of Yorktown in 1781. To join with General Washington, Rochambeau's armies came down all the way from Newport, Rhode Island, to the York River, in Virginia, and combined with Admiral François-Joseph-Paul de Grasse's fleet of French ships, which bottled the British ships. The French military action resulted in Cornwallis's surrender.[6]

That extraordinary, primordial gift of both money and manpower, military power and genius, helped pave the way for American independence. It set the stage for long-term reciprocities that endure today, despite occasional troubles growing out of cultural differences in the way we and the French view gifts and respond to those gifts.

An 1889 history text on France written by an American, David H. Montgomery, is a rare recognition of the American debt to France: "In her zeal for the cause of America, France seemed for a time to forget her own misery, and bankrupt though she was, she raised nine millions of francs as a gift to assist the armies of the new-born republic, besides furnishing about fifteen millions more as a loan. In addition . . . the Marquis de Lafayette, a young man of 20, loaded a vessel with arms and munitions of war at his own expense, and sailed for America to offer his services to General Washington."[7]

French contributions were not only financial and logistical. The thought of French philosopher Jean-Jacques Rousseau was embodied in the affirmation of the Declaration of Independence that "all men are created equal." The French officers and soldiers who fought under the American flag returned home inspired with a revolutionary zeal, thus restoring Rousseau's influence to France, after it had been tested and made operational in the New World. Still, Louis XVI, having inherited the burden of the exhausting wars fought by Louis XIV and Louis XV, incurred a debt of $1.3 billion in his war with England on behalf of America. Republican ideas and money crises drove the French Revolution that followed. (The French have never forgotten that their monarchy was weakened by the money that Louis XVI and his officers spent on those New World battles, thereby triggering the Revolution.) Similarly, republican ideas were to motivate Edouard-René Lefebvre de Laboulaye decades later in proposing the Statue of Liberty as a gift from France to celebrate the centennial of the July 4 Declaration of Independence.

The late great French historian, Fernand Braudel, (1902–85) shared with me, in various conversations in France and in the United States, his views of history as a series of long-term increments, little bits and pieces of human experience not necessarily related to changes in dynastic rule or wars or revolutions.[8] Thus a Maussian view of more than two hundred years of French-American relationships would require consideration of both a big picture of symbolic gift exchange and snapshots of smaller, lesser-known exchanges. For example, in 1778 France became the first nation to salute an American man-of-war ship, the *Ranger*, commanded by John Paul Jones. Americans later gave to France the ship *America*. After Lafayette fought on the colonialists' side and helped Franklin and Jefferson, a grateful United States gave him a land grant in Louisiana in 1803, and Congress voted to give him $200,000 and a Florida township during his 1824 return visit. Such small reciprocities are interspersed with the big ones: the Louisiana Purchase (made for such a "good price" that fifteen states were formed from the region, thus doubling the size of the country); the Statue of Liberty; military aid in two world wars; and the Marshall Plan. History has yet to pass judgment on the mutuality of EuroDisneyland.

Transactions between heads of state and exchanges in a highly personalized form make up a tapestry of gifts and obligations, both conscious and implicit, that continues to interact with other influences on the way we think, dress, eat, romance, assess each other's "national character," and form alliances. We find a good example of the fusion of personal and national identities in General Charles de Gaulle's restoring France's sense of grandeur in the twentieth century. His was a heroic effort to repair reciprocity after the long periods of damaged self-esteem brought on by war, military occupation, and debts. Gaullist citizens identifying with their leader felt better for his actions, thus completing a circuit linking individuals with the nation.[9] De Gaulle reached far back in time to restore that sense of grandeur, France's *mission civilisatrice*, and made Frenchmen proud to be reminded of another historian's (François Guizot's) observation that "there is hardly any great idea, hardly any great principle of civilization, which has not had to pass through France in order to be disseminated."[10] Yorktown and the Statue of Liberty then were part of recent French memory, links in a chain of history going back to the Roman conquest of Gaul.

I mentioned earlier that French historical consciousness contrasts with our own inventory of who owes to whom and what needs to be repaid. History is important to us, too, but our time perspective is distorted by a deliberate desire to start afresh, a tabula rasa attitude befitting what early settlers perceived as an empty continent. If history is to a nation what memory is to an individual, we Americans suffer occasional amnesia about what we owe to others. We prefer the roles of donor and teacher to those of recipient and pupil.

For example, the bicentennial of the Battle of Yorktown was vividly anticipated in France and almost totally ignored in the United States until the Smithsonian Institution was urged by the American ambassador to France, Arthur Hartman, to compensate for the indifference he was finding in the White House, the Department of State, and Congress. Hartman advised us to prepare our republic for a celebration that would live up to French expectations. "Each time I see President Giscard d'Estaing," the ambassador told me, "he asks what we are doing to prepare for October 18, 1981, and I am embarrassed to have no answers." Through a last-minute convening of interested parties, who met on neutral turf at the Smithsonian, and with the considerable influence of a historically minded Secretary of the Army, the Honorable John O. Marsh, Jr., and the Daughters of the American Revolution, Smithsonian Secretary S. Dillon Ripley and I managed to set a number of commemorations in motion.

Newly elected President Reagan finally invited newly elected

President Mitterrand to speak in Yorktown, along with Lord Hail-sham of Britain, who was sought especially to add some humor to the occasion. William H. G. FitzGerald and Francis Hodsoll of the White House helped raise private funds for a documentary film, for the hospitality in Yorktown shown to the French soldiers and sailors participating in the reenactment, and for the Smithsonian exhibition "By Land and by Sea: Independence with the Help of France." Such ad hoc approaches to remembering and fulfilling our historic obligations contrast sharply with the timetables of history guarded by, say, the French Ministry of Culture and a well-educated citizenry with a collective memory. French citizens living in Washington helped keep alive our awareness of French contributions through such organizations as the Lafayette-Rochambeau Society. They provided leadership in erecting at the battlefield site a temporary equestrian statue of General Washington, Rochambeau, and Lafayette by the sculptor Felix W. de Welden.

Marcel Mauss articulates his proposition that one is obliged to receive what is given as follows: "To refuse to give . . . is like refusing to accept—the equivalent of a declaration of war; it is a refusal of friendship and intercourse."[11] For various internal reasons, the Americans (mainly New Yorkers) organized to receive the Statue of Liberty, like those offering it, had good reason to value it. The New York Union League and later the Century Association became the locus of American efforts to create the American Committee, to secure the site and to oversee the construction, installation, and dedication. Bartholdi, the statue's creator, knew some members of the league and was aware of its commitment to both nationalism and art. Mobilizing the American public to embrace the statue as a symbol of national heritage became the goal of such visionary and pragmatic citizens as John Jay, Richard Butler, William Evarts, James W. Pinchot, Joseph Iasigi, Theodore Weston, Samuel Babcock, Nathan Appleton, Jr., Joseph Drexel, and many others up and down the coast from Boston to Philadelphia. Beauty and symbol became allied with function (it was to serve as a beacon or signal station) and commerce, argued some of the members, who also were eager to celebrate the early and lasting friendship of the two great republics of the nineteenth century. Moreover, the Statue of Liberty would glorify obliquely the preservation of the Union, being created so soon after the Civil War. Bartholdi, aware of the pacific significance of the statue, and not wishing to have his work rub salt in the wounds of the Confederacy, eliminated the Phyrigian bonnet and downplayed the broken chains that had appeared in earlier versions.

RETURNING THE GIFT:
THE TORTOISE AND THE HARE

Miss Liberty's American patrons, however, ran into huge difficulties in raising the money needed to build the pedestal on which the statue would rest—the American part of the arrangement to give and to receive. Richard H. Hunt, designer of some New Yorkers' urban palaces and Newport "cottages," the first American to graduate from l'école des Beaux-Arts, had been commissioned to design the pedestal. The task prompted much contentious give-and-take between Hunt and Bartholdi, so that their collaboration also can be understood as uneasy gift exchange in a microcosm.[12]

The pedestal became a symbol in itself for the American obligation to give something to match the French gift. Delays in finding money for it prompted vivid cartoon imagery. An anonymous artist shows Liberty lying on her back, with a floppy-eared Bugs Bunny creature labeled "France" standing guard while awaiting a slow-moving tortoise labeled "Collection Committee" and weighed down by granite slabs identified as "Bartholdi Pedestal?" *Frank Leslie's Illustrated Newspaper* in 1884 shows a toothless, haggard, and decrepit Statue of Liberty, torch and document-bearing arms dropped wearily to her side. Her rays of light are bent and drooping. Birds are shown nesting in the collection box near the first block of the cornerstone. Title: "Statue of Liberty, One Thousand Years Later, Waiting." President Cleveland vetoed federal funds for the pedestal as unconstitutional, but happily presided over the opening ceremony two years later. Americans were not yet accustomed to public subscription as a means of funding sculpture. The Bunker Hill Monument in Boston was not erected until eighteen years after the cornerstone was laid, and Congress had to appropriate money to complete the Washington Monument after the Civil War. Squabbling was rampant over whether the nation, the state, or the city was responsible.

Joseph Pulitzer, fresh from Budapest in 1863, came to the pedestal's rescue. Building on strong earlier support from the American Committee of the Sons of the American Revolution, Pulitzer launched a fundraising crusade through his newspaper, the *New York World*, and successfully raised more than $100,000 in five months' time. He listed names of all contributors. Bartholdi's personal letters to other newspapers were intended to help demonstrate the power of the press in generating public support for the pedestal. Parisian journals saw the delay in raising funds for the pedestal as a lack of American enthusiasm for the statue; one suggested that Liberty stay home and be erected at Le Havre.

Pulitzer's passionate editorial in 1885 reminded Americans of the broad base of French generosity and challenged them to match it. "The $250,000 that the making of the Statue cost was paid in by the masses of the French people—the working men, the tradesmen, the shopgirls, the artisans—by all, irrespective of class or condition. Let us respond in like manner. Let us not wait for the millionaires to give this money." So the committee collected $121,000 from 121,000 people, as Pulitzer bombarded the millionaires with insults—"a poor man's chance to one-up the rich."[13] American honor was saved. However, except for scholars, few Americans I know today seem aware of Pulitzer's role, concentrating instead on his Pulitzer prizes. If America's "common people" who contributed to the statue's pedestal did transmit the stories of it to their descendants, I find few traces of even folkloric memory among fellow citizens today. One encyclopedia, *World Book*, contains no reference at all to Pulitzer's contribution to the Liberty project. Similar discontinuities in recorded memory may prevail in France, but I doubt it. Polling could help verify or deny my hunch. Small but vital details are overshadowed by colossal statues once they are in place and take on a life of their own, independent of their creators or patrons. The National Park Service exhibition at the base of the Statue of Liberty begins to give Pulitzer his due.

Could it be that our national "amnesia" (i.e., about what our nation owes to others) also is related to a culturally determined aversion to being obligated or dependent? Through earlier religious influences, we have developed the notion that it is more blessed to give than to receive, and from our legal system we have derived a tendency to be suspicious of gifts. This suspicion of gift giving is illustrated in Kenneth L. Burns's 1985 documentary on the statue, quoting from the *New York Times* during the campaign in the 1880s to finance the statue's pedestal. The newspaper offered this anonymous quote: "It is ridiculous for Frenchmen to continue to impose on Americans a present they refuse to accept, to worry them with a souvenir that offends them, to humiliate them with a generous idea they do not comprehend, and to beg for thanks that they will not give."

Political campaigns in the United States typically reinforce the commonplace accusations leveled at candidates who accept gifts, incur obligations, and show special favors to their patrons. No other society is so permeated with the concept of "conflict of interest." Yet we are quick to charge others with ingratitude when, after we make a gift overseas, the recipient is found not to be amenable to our wishes.[14] French reactions to the United States Marshall Plan after World War II included popular support for General Charles de Gaulle for his fierce autonomy, which I have compared to "nativistic revivals" in simpler societies. De Gaulle is an example of a leader who emerges to restore a balance of reciprocity and self-esteem vis-à-vis benefactors who do not attach value to what the recipients want to give back.

The Statue of Liberty remains the archetype of a gift offered, a gift received, and a gift "repaid" through two world wars and the Marshall Plan. Healthy alliances are built on the capacity of one donor to reverse the role and become a recipient, and then to give again. As the United States has become a debtor nation through borrowing, and no longer can support an autonomous economy, Americans are having to learn such role reversals.

Happily, some educational endeavors are beginning to teach important history lessons. Two museums have been established to focus on the historic process of Franco-American giving, receiving, repaying. The first is the Musée Blérancourt, founded in 1924 at a seventeenth-century château eighty miles north of Paris. Anne Morgan, daughter of financier J. P. Morgan, whose bank loans to France were repaid, first bought the property in 1917 and made it her headquarters for helping the wounded and homeless in France after World War I. Later, she used the château as a private museum to memorialize mutual aid between France and the United States, and in 1930 she gave the château and her collections to the French government. It is known today as the French National Museum of Franco-American Friendship.

Starting with naval and military battles in which France fought, principally Yorktown, the Blérancourt exhibition treats the great

French and American heroes—Washington, Lafayette, Rochambeau, Grasse, John Paul Jones, and others—before focusing on the
Treaty of Paris of 1783, which ended the American Revolution.
Other themes deal with the British and the French presence in the
New World before the Revolution; how American ideas influenced
the French Revolution; the Treaty of 1802; the Louisiana sale; the
French presence in the United States around 1800 as well as during
the rule of Napoleon III, manifested by Lafayette's famous tour, and
how we absorbed Bonapartist refugees. The Statue of Liberty is giv-
en attention in a pavilion devoted to "America: Land of Liberty."
Winding up the nineteenth century, the Musée Blérancourt exhibition takes note of the Industrial Revolution and its effects on both
countries, international exhibitions, and the French fascination for
American skyscrapers. Yet another pavilion exhibits artworks by
American artists in France and French artists in America.

The historic Laboulaye family continues to have a hand in the
museum, starting with Ambassador André de Laboulaye, a contemporary of Anne Morgan's, and his son, Ambassador François de
Laboulaye, the Washington-born diplomat who followed in his father's footsteps, representing France in Washington during the bicentennial at Yorktown and preparing the way for the centennial
celebration of the Statue of Liberty.

A second museum that focuses on Franco-American gift exchange is the Statue of Liberty National Monument at Liberty Island, administered by the National Park Service. "The Gift of
Friendship" is the banner at the top of a brochure given to today's
visitors to the exhibition area of the Statue of Liberty National Museum. Designed by the firm of Chermayoff and Geisman, the exhibition explains how the colossal figure of a woman striding with up-
lifted flame across the entrance to the New World has become a
symbol of America to most people, including Americans. Visitors
also can learn that Liberty Enlightening the World was conceived
as an expression of French republican ideals, initiated in 1865 by
Edouard de Laboulaye, a legal scholar and authority on America.
Laboulaye chafed under the repressive regime of Napoleon III and
looked admiringly at the United States, a thriving republic that had
just survived a civil war and was on the threshold of becoming a
prosperous industrial nation. He admired, says the brochure, a nation that had "achieved a delicate balance between liberty and sta-

bility that for so long had eluded France." He knew that the statue would be considered subversive inside France, and left it to the gifted Bartholdi to help make Liberty a reality.

Though not a museum, EuroDisneyland features more than Mickey Mouse. The Liberty and Discovery arcade celebrates the creation of the Statue of Liberty, from Bertholdi to the rebirth of Lady Liberty in 1986. This American tribute to the gift may offset some French objections to the Paris-area theme park as a "cultural Chernobyl."

In the more than a century since Liberty became our national icon, the country has passed through earlier objections from the clergy that France had offered us a pagan goddess or else a fatted calf, or that Liberty, with all her Masonic symbols, represented a secret Masonic plot. Various other citizens have dared to look "the gift horse in the mouth." As late as 1925, a Paris newspaper reported that an American pastor, the Reverend Doctor Andrew Bard, had suggested that the Statue of Liberty be replaced by a statue of Christ. The newspaper then added this editorial comment:

> Alas, 1,925 years have passed since the son of God vainly tried to illuminate the conscience of man without success. No. The idea of . . . Dr. Bard is not tenable. We would understand a statue later of Senator LaFollette, or that of a dry America holding a Bible and surrounding by customs officials. We could accept the project of a colossal cowboy, dancing girl, Dempsey or Rockefeller—in short, anything "exciting"—but a statue of Christ, so poor among the poor, erected at the entrance of the country of the dollar and temple of money? No . . . [s]uch a statue would be capable, all by itself, of slipping away in a day when the White House, influenced by Wall Street bankers, would demand from creditors a little interest for having taken part in the great war for humanity.[15]

Such use of stereotypes and candor by the French can be analyzed as signs of both an enduring and possessive pride in having made such a gift[16] and an intimacy between two quite different peoples who have become "family."

If we move beyond diplomacy, strategy, economics, and intellectual influences over two centuries of history and think of the intangible yet fundamental plane of sentiment and attraction, we will feel as French historian Jean-Baptiste Duroselle did when he wrote,

Fig. 9.6. President Franklin D. Roosevelt, flanked by military aides, celebrating the fiftieth anniversary of the Statue of Liberty at Liberty Island in 1936. Reprinted by permission of National Park Service, Statue of Liberty National Monument.

"I do not hesitate to say it: Franco-American relations have never lost the mysterious charm that assures them a place apart in the history of mankind."[17]

Like a great Rorschach test, Liberty has attracted all kinds of interpretations and meanings at different periods of national and world history. A whole book could be written on the perceptions revealed by ceremonial oratory marking the arrival and dedication of the gift in 1886, followed by the fiftieth, seventy-fifth, and hundredth anniversaries. Comparisons and contrasts could be found in the French oratory crafted for those same occasions. One indicator of the overwhelming success of the French gift is the degree to which the statue speaks to differing self-images and national needs of the American people.

At the fiftieth anniversary celebration in 1936, Franklin D. Roosevelt recalled what Grover Cleveland had said half a century earlier on the same spot: "We will not forget that liberty has made here her home ... nor shall her chosen altar be neglected" (fig. 9.6).[18] FDR then used what turned out to be prophetic language, as the United States was already having to face the challenge of Hitler and the need for national unity to fight that future war: "The realization that we are all bound together by hope of a common future

Fig. 9.7. Pencil sketch by Richard E. Stamm, Keeper of the Castle Collection at the Smithsonian Institution. This bronze replica of the Statue of Liberty stands on l'Ile des Cygnes, an island in the Seine River, downstream from the Eiffel Tower. The American community of Paris donated the replica as a gift to France. The Eiffel Tower was completed in 1889, three years after the Statue of Liberty opened. French engineer Gustave Eiffel designed both the Eiffel Tower and the interior structure that supports the Statue of Liberty.

rather than reverence for a common past has helped us to build on this continent a unity unapproached . . . in the whole world. . . . For all our millions of square miles . . . and people, there is a unity in language and speech, in law and economics, in education and in general purpose, which nowhere finds its match."[19]

In the last decade of this century, amid unprecedented ethnic fragmentation, the United States can discover some gifts in the oratory of earlier leaders as we try to rediscover what myths and symbols we hold in common while preserving and celebrating our diversity and our multiple identities. The worldwide commemoration of the 250th anniversary of the birth of Thomas Jefferson in 1993 will provide such an opportunity.

The Statue of Liberty continues her ad valorem mission, bestowing on the world "added value," enriching the donor and the recipient nation together and, indeed, the entire world. On July 4, 1889, the American community in Paris offered the French people a gift of a bronze replica of the Statue of Liberty; it still stands now, on an island in the Seine River, downstream from the Eiffel Tower (fig. 9.7). In a symbolic sense, this recently restored American gift closes the circle of gift giving that was launched by the French in the 1860s with the gift of Miss Liberty. In a deeper sense, though, the American replica in Paris serves to extend and strengthen the chain of reciprocity between the two peoples that has existed since before the founding of the American Republic and that promises to continue well into the future.

This magnificent exchange of gifts illustrates a declaration delivered by French ambassador Jules J. Jusserand on the occasion of the 1916 ceremony at which Liberty's torch was first lighted with electricity: "Not to a man, not to a nation, the statue was raised. It was raised to an idea—an idea greater than France or the United States: the idea of Liberty."[20]

Contrast that with the Trojan horse!

NOTES

1. A massive mockup of the Trojan horse, made of wood, stands at the entrance of the legendary archaeological site in Hisarlik, Turkey, where tourists may now examine layers of centuries of Greco-Roman cultures. John Fleischman's magazine article "'I Sing of Gods and Men'—and the Stones of Fabled Troy" (*Smithsonian* 22, no. 10 [January 1992]) foreshadowed his current book project about Troy and the human imagination.

2. Victor Turner, the mentor of Barbara Babcock and John MacAloon, whose essay appears in this volume, drew heavily on history and literature in his anthropological career. His *Forest of Symbols*, based on his studies of an African tribe, was published by Cornell University Press in 1967.

3. An example of the domestication of the Statue of Liberty can be found in the Washington private residence of President Woodrow Wilson, now administered by the National Trust for Historic Preservation. A rug depicting American scenes features the Statue of Liberty, the Liberty Bell, the *Mayflower*, Independence Hall, and the Washington Monument, among other notable "native" sites. The rug lies in Wilson's study and served as a reminder to him, during his long convalescence, of his having presided over the electrification of the statue's beacon in 1916.

4. Originally published as "Essai sur le don, forme et raison de l'échange dans les sociétés archaïques," in *L'Année Sociologique* (1923–24), and given a much wider audience in Claude Lévi-Strauss, ed., *Sociologie et Anthropologie* (Paris: Presses Universitaires de France, 1850); Mauss's ideas eventually reached the English-speaking world in 1954 with a translation by Ian Cunnison, *The Gift* (Glencoe, Ill.: Free Press, 1954).

5. Wilton S. Dillon, *Gifts and Nations: The Obligation to Give, Receive, and Repay*, with a foreword by Talcott Parsons (The Hague and Paris: Mouton, 1968). I discovered Mauss through Lévi-Strauss in Paris in 1951. Decades later, I found Mauss highly relevant to understanding the Statue of Liberty as a key to the gift exchange metaphor in international relations.

6. Howard C. Rice, Jr., and Anne S. K. Brown, trans. and eds., *The American Campaigns of Rochambeau's Army 1780, 1781, 1782, 1783* (Princeton, N.J.: Princeton University Press and Providence, R.I.: Brown University Press, 1972).

7. David H. Montgomery, *The Leading Facts of French History* (Boston: Ginn, 1889).

8. "The short-term is the most capricious and deceptive form of time," Braudel wrote in "History and the Social Sciences," in *Economy and Society in Early Modern Europe: Essays from Annales*, edited by Peter Burke (New York: Harper, 1958). Braudel would have had much to say about contrasting time perspectives of the French and the Americans; the Statue of Liberty indeed gives tangible expression to French preferences for the long term—a gift that lasts.

9. Individuals of different social classes whom I knew in France were attracted to Gaullism as a reminder that France could control her own destiny once again. In my essay "Bonne Année, Oncle Charles" (*New Republic*, January 4, 1964), I explained De Gaulle's independence as not "anti-American" but pro-French, still regarding us as *en famille*, while he was cool and formal with the Soviets with whom he did not "fuss" as much.

10. François Guizot's eight-volume *History of France* (1789–1848) and six-volume *History of the Revolution in England* (1826–56) stimulated nineteenth-century historians to think comparatively of France and the "Anglo-Saxons." David H. Montgomery was a good example.

11. Mauss, *The Gift*, 11.

12. For a richly textured account of that relationship from the perspective of architectural history, see Marvin Trachtenberg, "The Pedestal," in his *Statue of Liberty* (New York: Penguin, 1986). How Bartholdi and Hunt evolved their conceptions for the pedestal is beautifully illustrated in Susan

R. Stein, "Richard Morris Hunt and the Pedestal," in *Liberty: The French-American Statue in Art and History*, catalog for a traveling exhibition of the New York Public Library and the Comité officiel Franco-Américain pour la célébration centenaire de la Statue de la Liberté (New York: Harper and Row, 1986).

13. Cf. June Hargrove, "The Power of the Press," in *Liberty*.

14. Some French recipients of Marshall Plan benefits wished we had made the gift with a confession that it also served American self-interest; such an acknowledgment would have reduced their sense of indebtedness to the United States. What we implied as our hope for "repayment" was anti-Communist votes, permission to station troops, and gratitude. None of the above corresponded to what the French wanted from us: recognition of their earlier contributions to us, especially the Battle of Yorktown and the Statue of Liberty; consultations about French achievements in research and development during wartime; and acceptance of French knowledge about how to deal with the Islamic world from which we were trying to remove the French. Cf. my *Gifts and Nations* and "Allah Loves Strong Men," *Columbia University Forum* (Winter 1961).

15. Quoted in *New York Times*, July 20, 1925.

16. Bartholdi's pride was understandable when he declared: "It is a comfort to know that this statue will exist 1,000 years from now long after our names will be forgotten" (quoted in caption at exhibition at base of Statue of Liberty).

17. Cf. *France and the United States*, trans. Derek Coltman (Chicago and London: University of Chicago Press, 1978).

18. Text provided by Franklin D. Roosevelt Library, National Archives and Records Administration, Hyde Park, N.Y.

19. Ibid.

20. Cf. *New York Times*, December 3, 1916.

Bibliography

Editors' Note: The editors wish to acknowledge the work of Barry Moreno, librarian technician on the staff of the Statue of Liberty National Monument, in the preparation of this bibliography.

BOOKS

Aguila, Dani, comp. and ed. *Taking Liberty with the Lady, by Cartoonists around the World.* Nashville: Eagle Nest Publishing, 1986.

Allen, Leslie. *Liberty: The Statue and the American Dream.* New York: Statue of Liberty–Ellis Island Foundation, 1985.

Baker, Paul R. *Richard Morris Hunt.* Cambridge, Mass., and London: MIT Press, 1980.

Bartholdi, Frédéric-Auguste. *The Statue of "Liberty Enlightening the World" As Described by the Sculptor.* New York: North American Review Press, 1885.

Bartholdi Souvenir: A Sketch of the Colossal Statue Presented by France to the United States. New York: Farrell and Everdell, 1886.

Bell, James B., and Richard I. Abrams. *In Search of Liberty: The Story of the Statue of Liberty and Ellis Island.* Garden City, N.Y.: Doubleday, 1984.

Betz, Jacques. *Bartholdi.* Paris: Editions de Minuit, 1954.

Bigelow, John. *Some Recollections of the Late Edouard de Laboulaye.* New York: G. P. Putnam's Sons, 1888.

Blanchet, Christian, and Bertrand Dard. *Statue of Liberty: The First Hundred Years.* Translated from the French by Bernard A. Weisberger. New York: American Heritage Press, 1985.

Boime, Albert. *Hollow Icons: The Politics of Sculpture in XIXth-Century France.* Kent, O., and London: Kent State University Press, 1987.

Burchard, Sue. *The Statue of Liberty: Birth to Rebirth.* New York: Harcourt, Brace, Jovanovich, 1985.

Chapman, G. *The Third Republic of France, the First Phase, 1871–1891.* London, 1962.

Chen, Tsing-fang. *The Spirit of Liberty.* New York: Lucia Gallery, 1986.

Cobban, Alfred. *A History of Modern France.* Harmondsworth, Eng.: Viking Penguin, 1965.

Depew, Chauncey Mitchell. *Oration by the Honorable Chauncey M. Depew at the Unveiling of Bartholdi's Statue of Liberty Enlightening the World.* New York: De Vinne Press, 1886.

Farre, F., ed. *Union franco-américaine: Discours de Messieurs Henri Martin, E. B. Washburne, E. de Laboulaye, et J. W. Forney.* Paris, 1875.

Faucher, J. A. *Histoire de la franco-maçonnerie en France.* Paris, 1967.

Fiore, Mercia. *The Lady behind the Light.* River Grove, Ill.: Fiore Enterprises, 1985.

Fisher, Leonard Everett. *The Statue of Liberty.* New York: Holiday House, 1985.

Fox, Mary Virginia. *The Statue of Liberty.* New York: Julian Messner, 1985.

Garnett, John J. *The Statue of Liberty: Its History, Conception, Construction, and Inauguration.* New York: B. W. Dinsmore, 1886.

Gautier, Claude. *La Statue de la Liberté: Un Signe pour vous.* Editions ABC. Nîmes, France: Les Presses de Castellum, 1986.

Gilder, Rodman. *The Statue of Liberty Enlightening the World.* New York: New York Trust Company, 1943.

Gooch, George Peabody. *The Second Empire.* London, 1960.

Grumet, Michael. *Images of Liberty.* New York: Arbour House, 1986.

Gschaedler, André. *True Light on the Statue of Liberty and Its Creator.* Narberth, Pa.: Livingston Publishing Company, 1966.

Handlin, Oscar. *Statue of Liberty.* New York: Newsweek Books, 1971.

Harris, Jonathan. *A Statue for America: The First 100 Years of the Statue of Liberty.* New York: Four Winds Press, 1985.

Hayden, Richard, and Thierry Despont. *Restoring the Statue of Liberty.* New York: McGraw-Hill, 1986.

Holliman, Jennie. *The History of the Statue of Liberty, Part II.* Washington, D.C.: National Park Service, 1934.

Hughes, Regina M. *The History of the Statue of Liberty, Part I.* Washington, D.C.: National Park Service, 1934.

The Inauguration of the Statue of 'Liberty Enlightening the World' by the President of the United States and Count de Lesseps on Bedloe's Island. New York: D. Appleton, 1886.

Jacob, H. E. *The World of Emma Lazarus.* New York: Schocken Books, 1949.

Kallop, Jr., Edward L., comp. *Images of Liberty: Models and Reductions of the Statue of Liberty 1867–1917.* New York: Christie, Manson, and Woods International, 1985.

Kraske, Robert. *The Statue of Liberty Comes to America.* Champaign, Ill.: Garrard, 1972.

Laboulaye, Edouard-René de. *Histoire des Etats-Unis.* 3 vols. Paris, 1855–66.

———. *Paris en Amérique.* Paris, 1863.

Lami, S. *Dictionnaire des sculpteurs de l'école française au dix-neuvième siècle.* Paris, 1914–21.

Lemoine, Bertrand. *La Statue de la Liberté.* Bruxelles et Liège, Royaume de Belge: Mardaga, Institut Français de l'Architecture, 1986.

Levine, Benjamin. *The History of Bedloe's Island.* New York: New York University Press, 1952.

———. *The Statue of Liberty National Monument.* Washington, D.C.: National Park Service, 1952.

Levinson, Nancy Smiler. *I Lift My Lamp: Emma Lazarus and the Statue of Liberty.* New York: E. P. Dutton, Lodestar Books, 1986.

Maestro, Giulio, and Betsy Maestro. *The Story of the Statue of Liberty.* New York: William Morrow, 1986.

Marrey, Bertrand. *La Vie et l'oeuvre extraordinaires de Monsieur Gustave Eiffel.* Paris: Graphite, 1984.

Mercer, Charles. *Statue of Liberty.* New York: G. P. Putnam's Sons, 1979.

Merriam, Eve. *Emma Lazarus: Woman with a Torch.* New York: Citadel Press, 1956.

Michael, George. *The Statue of Liberty.* New York: Abrams, 1985.

Nash, Margo. *Statue of Liberty: Keeper of Dreams.* Glendale, N.Y.: Berry Enterprises, 1983.

Nason, Thelma. *Our Statue of Liberty.* Chicago: Follett Publishing, 1969. Reissued. Cleveland, O.: Modern Curriculum Press, 1986.

New York Public Library and Comité officiel Franco-Américain pour la célébration centenaire de la Statue de la Liberté, with Pierre Provoyeur and June Hargrove. *Liberty: The French-American Statue in Art and History.* New York: Harper and Row, 1986.

Pauli, Hertha Ernestine. *Gateway to America: Miss Liberty's First Hundred Years.* New York: David McKay; distributed by Random House, 1965.

———, and E. B. Ashton. *I Lift My Lamp: The Way of a Symbol.* New York: Ira J. Friedman, Inc., and Appleton-Century, 1948. Reissued in 1969.

Perrault, Carole. *The Statue of Liberty and Liberty Island: A Chronicle of the Physical Conditions and Appearance of the Island, 1871–1956.* North Atlantic Historic Preservation Centre, National Park Service, 1984.

Pitkin, Thomas. *Prospectus of the American Museum of Immigration at the Statue of Liberty National Monument*. Washington, D.C.: National Park Service, 1956.

Porter, Fitzjohn. *In Memory of General Stone*. New York, 1890.

Price, W. *Bartholdi and the Statue of Liberty*. Chicago, 1959.

Rogers, Frances. *Big Miss Liberty*. New York: Frederick A. Stokes, 1938.

Romigh, Philip S. *Fort Wood: Statue of Liberty National Monument*. Denver Source Center, National Park Service, 1973.

Schmitt, Jean-Marie. *Bartholdi: Une Certaine Idée de la Liberté*. Strasbourg, France: Editions de la Nuée-bleue, 1985.

———. *Colmar: Its Monuments and Its Architecture, from the Beginning to 1914*. 1983.

Schneider, Dick. *Freedom's Holy Light*. Nashville: Nelson, 1985.

Shapiro, Mary J. *How They Built the Statue of Liberty*. New York: Random House, 1985.

Shapiro, William. *The Statue of Liberty*. New York: Franklin Watts, 1985.

Smaridge, Nora. *The Tallest Lady in the World: The Statue of Liberty*. New York: Hawthorne Books, 1967.

Stein, Susan P., ed. *The Architecture of Richard Morris Hunt*. Chicago: The University of Chicago Press, 1986.

Stoddard, Seneca Roy. *The Statue of 'Liberty Enlightening the World.'* Glens Falls, New York, 1891.

Stone, Ross Conway. *A Way to See and Study the Statue of Liberty Enlightening the World*. New York: Bullion Publishing, 1887.

Story, I. F. *The Statue of Liberty*. Historical Handbook Series, no. 11. Washington, D.C.: National Park Service, 1961.

Trachtenberg, Marvin. *The Statue of Liberty*. New York: Viking, 1976. Reprint. Harmondsworth, Eng.: Penguin, 1977.

Webster, Nesta. *The French Revolution*. Costa Mesa, Calif.: Noontide Press, 1988. Originally published in 1919.

Weinbaum, Paul. *The Statue of Liberty: Heritage of America*. Las Vegas: KC Publications, 1979.

Wilmot, Lisa. *Fort Eleazar Wood: Foundation of Liberty*. Washington, D.C.: National Park Service, 1977.

ARTICLES

Agnew, J. C. "Miss Liberty in Triplicate." *New York Times Magazine*, January 7, 1945, 22.

"America's Lady Liberty Gets More Than a Facelift." *Design News* 40 (September 17, 1984): 18–19.

"Anniversary of the Statue of Liberty." *Mentor* 13 (October 1925): 49.

"The Architecture of Richard Morris Hunt." Book Review. *Library Journal,* May 1, 1986, 114.

"Arrival of the Statue of Liberty." *Scientific American* 62 (June 1885): 400.

Auchincloss, Louis. "Building on the Past: The Statue of Liberty Pedestal." *New York,* May 12, 1986, 86.

"Auguste Bartholdi's Last Monument." *American Architect* 86 (October 1904): 63.

"Bannon and the Lady." *Popular Photography* 92 (January 1985): 84.

"Bartholdi's Statue of Liberty." Parts 1 and 2. *American Architect and Building News* 4 (December 1878): 77–78; 14 (November 1883): 126–27, 137–38.

"Bartholdi Statue." *Harper's New Monthly Magazine* 71 (August 1885): 475.

"Beauty Treatment for Miss Liberty." *Literary Digest* 111 (December 1931): 25.

Benét, James. "Mother of Exiles." *New Republic* 89 (November 25, 1936): 108–9.

Benét, William Rose. "Liberty and Hot Dogs." *Saturday Review of Literature* 4 (June 30, 1928): 997.

Brock, H. I. "Liberty's New Dress." *New York Times Magazine,* July 4, 1948, 12.

Browne, M. "Liberty Enlightening Paris: The Replica of the Statue of Liberty on the Isle of Swans." *Christian Science Monitor,* June 17, 1936, 3.

Carlson, Peter. "Restorers Place Her under Intensive Care." *People* 220 (July 9, 1984): 61.

Clark, M. "Let the Lady Speak: Programmes of Welcome." *Christian Science Monitor Weekly Magazine,* September 15, 1945, 5.

Edward, C. "Unveiling of a Great Lady." *American History and Illustrations* 14 (May 1979): 10–15.

Ehrlich, B. "The Lady We Can Not Afford to Forget." *Saturday Evening Post* 220 (January 17, 1948): 30–31.

Emerson, G. "Statue of Liberty." *Holiday* 22 (December 1957): 51.

"Emma Lazarus: A Poetess of Exile and Freedom." *Christian Century* 19 (November 1986): 1033.

"England and the Great Statue." *Harper's Weekly* 30 (October 1886): 727.

"Facelift Ahead after Century." *U.S. News and World Report* 95 (August 1, 1983): 8.

"Face of the U.S.A." *Collier's* 123 (January 22, 1949): 24–25.

"Fade Out, Fade In: Some Players in the Passing Parade." Pictorial Review of the Year 1984. *Life* 8 (January 1985): 49–54.

Farley, B. "Liberty Enlightening the World." *National Education Association Journal* 24 (November 1935): 245.

"Favourite Lady Makes a Comeback." *Engineering News-Record* 213 (July 5, 1984): 32–39.

"Floodlighting the Statue of Liberty." *American City* 60 (September 1945): 151.

Foley, L. "Simple Exercise in Cultural Correlation." *School and Society* 56 (December 5, 1942).

"From Torch to Toe: A Kid's-Eye View of Miss Liberty's Restoration." *Instructor* 94 (October 1984): 32–35.

Galbraith, R. "Rosy Setting for a Famous Lady." *Life* 42 (February 11, 1957): 6–7.

"A Giant Task: Cleaning the Statue of Liberty." *Popular Mechanics* 57 (February 1932): 203–5.

Gibson, Henry. "Bartholdi in Philadelphia." *Philadelphia Magazine,* October 1986, 89.

"Girl and Birds." *New Yorker* 35 (October 3, 1959): 36.

"Give Me Your Well-Heeled." *Forbes* 131 (April 11, 1983): 184.

Golden, F. "Lady in a Cage." *Discover* 5 (July 1984): 18–25.

Gould, K. M. "Golden Door." *Scholastic* 66 (February 9, 1955): 15.

Halter, John C. "Giving Liberty a Hand." *Boys' Life* 74 (July 1984): 17–19.

Hazzard, Shirley. "The Statue and the Bust." *McCall's* 98 (August 1971): 32.

Heidish, Marcy, and Peter B. Kaplan. "The Grande Dame of the Harbour." *Geo* 6 (July 1984): 36–45.

Heimberger, J. J. "The Statue of Liberty: An American Tradition. Plan for the Celebration of Its Fiftieth Anniversary." *School Life* 22 (October 1936): 35–36.

"Here and There: Bartholdi's France." *Travel-Holiday,* July 1985, 84.

Herzog, A. "Lure of Liberty." *New York Times Magazine,* October 22, 1961, 100–102.

"How a Great Memorial Was Made." *Travel* 91 (October 1948): 30.

Iacocca, Lee. "Lady Liberty Needs You." *Instructor* 92 (February 1983): 42.

"I Lift My Lamp beside the Golden Door." *American History (Illustrated),* June 1986, 30.

"The Illumination of Miss Liberty." *Outlook* 114 (December 13, 1916): 86–87.

"The Inauguration of the Statue of Liberty." *Scientific American* 55 (November 6, 1886): 288.

"Independent Extruder Fabricated Scaffold for Statue of Liberty." *Light Metal Age* 42 (June 1984): 34–35.

Kaplan, Peter, and Mary Carroll. "The Lady Lives." *National Parks and Conservation* 58 (May–June 1984): 10–11.

"Keeper of the Flame." *Reader's Digest* 120 (February 1982): 119–21.

"The Lady Gets a New Flame." *Fortune* 90 (August 1974): 168–69.

"Landing of a Landmark: From a Frenchman's Folly to an American Icon." *Liberty at One Hundred. Life,* July 1986, 50.

Lawson, L. "The Statue of Liberty? You're Kidding!" *Model Photography* 40 (February 1976): 86–87.

Lazarus, Emma. "The New Colossus." *New York Times Magazine*, July 4, 1948, 12.

Leach, Henry. "America and Liberty." *Living Age* 7, ser. 8 (July 1917): 48–53.

"Learning about Lady Liberty." *Instructor* 93 (February 1984): 52–56.

"Liberty Changing Inside Out." *Engineering News-Record* 212 (February 16, 1984): 13.

"Liberty Enlightening the World." *Scientific American* 52 (June 13, 1885): 375–76.

"Liberty in the Making." *UNESCO Courier* 29 (July 1976): 31–33.

"Liberty Needs a Helping Hand." *National Geographic World*, October 1984, 30.

"Liberty: Passing on the Torch." *Time* 124 (July 9, 1984): advertising supplement.

"Liberty Renovation Planned." *Engineering News-Record* 211 (July 28, 1983): 13.

"Liberty's Jubilee." *Time* 28 (November 9, 1936): 27–28.

"Liberty to Speak." *Scholastic* 27 (November 2, 1935): 16.

"Liberty under Repair." *Technology Review* 87 (July 1984): 62–69.

"Lighting Our Monuments." *Literary Digest* 54 (January 13, 1917): 67.

"Living Up to Liberty." *Outing* 59 (March 1917): 576–77.

"Living with a Goddess." *American Magazine* 159 (June 1955): 49.

McCullough, David G. "Hail Liberty!" *American Heritage* 17 (February 1966): 22–23.

Meta, M. "The Largest Statue in the World and How It Was Built." *Strand Magazine* 17 (December 1899): 770–74.

"Mighty Woman with a Torch." *Senior Scholastic* 85 (October 28, 1964): 7.

"Miss Liberty's Golden Jubilee." *Scholastic* 29 (October 17, 1936): 16.

"Moving the Statue of Liberty from New York to New Jersey." *Newsweek* 42 (December 21, 1953): 24.

"Moving the Statue of Liberty from New York to New Jersey." Response from C. P. Barnum. *Newsweek* 43 (January 18, 1954): 6.

"'The New Colossus': Tablet at the Base of the Statue of Liberty." *Scholastic* 36 (February 12, 1940): 11.

"New Floodlighting for Statue of Liberty." *American City* 46 (June 1932): 151.

"New Lights for Liberty." *American City* 57 (January 1942): 97.

Nielson, N. "Keeping the Torch Lit." *Materials Performance* 23 (April 1984): 78.

"Our Fair Lady: The Statue of Liberty." *Reader's Digest*, July 1986, 46.

"Our Great Goddess and Her Coming Idol." *American Catholic Quarterly Review* 5 (1880): 587–97.

"Our Number One Symbol." *New York Times Magazine,* June 22, 1941, 13.

Paris, L. "Mother of Exile." *Scholastic* 69 (January 11, 1957): 14.

Pauli, Hertha. "Golden Door." *Christian Science Monitor,* November 20, 1948, 2.

"Pedestal for the Statue of Liberty." *American Architect and Building News* 14 (December 1883): 253, 284–85.

Perry, Ralph Barton. "Uncle Sam and the Statue of Liberty." *Century* 107 (February 1924): 608–14.

"Pilgrimage to America's Most Famous Monument." *Life* 10 (June 2, 1941): 94–97.

Pizer, Vernon. "The Lady on Liberty Island." *American Legion* 111 (July 1981): 8–11.

Polk, J. "Poor Butterfly." *New Yorker* 17 (June 7, 1941): 24.

Postal, B., and L. Thoppman. "Liberty Stands on Her Words: Excerpts from American-Jewish Landmarks. A Travel Guide and History." *Ms.* 6 (August 1977): 22.

Poudim, N. "He Built the Statue of Liberty: Frédéric-Auguste Bartholdi." *Reader's Digest,* April 1977, 10, 27–32.

"Preserving Irreplaceable Landmarks." *House and Garden* 156 (January 1984): 161.

Rowsome, F. "When Liberty Was Imported." *American Mercury* 57 (July 1943): 72–79.

Rush, G. "Taking Care of Miss Liberty." An Interview with Superintendent David Moffitt. *Esquire,* July 1986, 72–74.

Russell, John. "A Face That Really Launched a Thousand Ships—and Many More." *Smithsonian* 15 (July 1984): 46–56.

"Saga of a Lady of Liberty." *New York Times Magazine,* July 5, 1959, 12–13.

Saunders, J. "Hospitality Demands Are Heavy for the Lady with the Torch." *Parks and Recreation* 4 (October 1969): 43–44.

"Sculpture Tells the Immigrant Story." *National Parks and Conservation* 56 (March–April 1982): 32–33.

"Statue la colossale: Report of a Lecture by Mr. Marvin Trachtenberg." *New Yorker* 53 (August 1, 1979): 15–16.

"Statue of Liberty Celebration—28 October 1936." *National Education Association Journal* 25, supp. 90 (September 1936).

"The Statue of Liberty." *Frank Leslie's Popular Monthly* 20 (August 1885): 129–44.

"The Statue of Liberty." *Harper's Weekly* 30 (October 30, 1886): 695.

"The Statue of Liberty Is Losing Her Girdle." *Engineering News-Record* 207 (December 3, 1981): 19.

"The Statue of Liberty Nearing Completion." *Scientific American* 65 (August 14, 1886): 100.

"The Statue of Liberty, New York." *Scientific American* 65 (November 20, 1886): 320.

"The Statue of Liberty: The Face That Met a Thousand Ships." *New Jersey Monthly* 6 (July 1982): 90.

"Statue of Liberty to Close Down for Repairs. $230 Million Needed to Restore Ellis Island." *National Parks Conservation* 57 (March-April 1983): 39.

"Taking Care of Miss Liberty." *Esquire* 98 (July 1982): 72–74.

Trachtenberg, Marvin. "Statue of Liberty: Transparent Banality or Avant-garde Conundrum?" *Art in America* 62 (May 1974): 36–43.

"Unveiling the Bartholdi Statue of Liberty." *Public Opinion* 2 (November 6, 1886): 69–71.

Virden, H. "Lady with a Torch." *Independent Woman* 27 (February 1948), inside cover.

Whittier, John Greenleaf. "The Bartholdi Statue." *Critic* 6 (November 6, 1886): 225.

William, A. "Lady of Liberty." *Coronet* 38 (August 1955): 110–12.

UNPUBLISHED MANUSCRIPTS

Unpublished manuscripts listed in the bibliography are in the collections at the Research Library, Statue of Liberty National Monument.

Blumberg, Barbara. "Celebrating the Immigrant: An Administrative History of the Statue of Liberty National Monument (Including the American Museum of Immigration at Liberty Island), 1952–1982." New York: Institute for Research in History.

Camp, Oswald E., Superintendent of the Statue of Liberty. "The Statue of Liberty National Monument." Fiftieth Anniversary Celebration, 1936. National Park Service, Washington, D.C., 1937.

Colabella, A. V. "Proposed Architectural and Engineering Agreement, Statue of Liberty." 1973.

Connor, John David. "Essaying on Liberty—With Regards to Topographics, Novelties, Proper Understanding and Commentary, Etc." Harvard Unversity, Cambridge, Mass., 1992.

Franco-American Committee for the Restoration of the Statue of Liberty. "The Statue of Liberty Report." Washington, D.C., 1983.

Greenstein, Robert. "A Summary of the Structural History of Fort Wood." Washington, D.C.: National Park Service, 1963.

Hageman, Samuel Miller. "The Goddess of Liberty at Her Unveiling in the Harbor of New York, October 28, 1886."

Hugins, Walter. "A Short History of the Statue of Liberty." Washington, D.C.: National Park Service, 1956.

Means, Georgia S. "Bedloe's Island and Fort Wood."

Moreno, Barry. "How the Statue of Liberty Became a National Monument." Unpublished manuscript. National Park Service, Washington, D.C., 1988.

Pitkin, Thomas. "Preliminary Draft of the Prospectus of the American Museum of Immigration, Liberty Island." Washington, D.C.: National Park Service, 1955.

———. "Summary of the Structural History of Fort Wood." Washington, D.C.: National Park Service, 1956.

Statue of Liberty–Ellis Island Foundation. "Centennial for Liberty, 1886–1986." New York, 1983.

Witte, Christian. "L'Isle de la Liberté: Piédestal pour une Idée, 1886–1986." 1986.

Contributors

BARBARA A. BABCOCK is professor of English and comparative cultural and literary studies at the University of Arizona in Tucson. Educated at Northwestern University and at The University of Chicago (Ph.D. in comparative literature, 1975), she has worked in the fields of anthropology, comparative literature, women's studies, folklore, and Native American studies. She served as director of the Pembroke Center for Teaching and Research on Women at Brown University and has taught at the University of Texas at Austin. A former member of the Institute for Advanced Study at Princeton University, she is the author of *The Pueblo Storyteller: Development of a Figurative Ceramic Tradition* (1986) and the coauthor (with Nancy Parezo) of *Daughters of the Desert: Women Anthropologists and the Native American Southwest, 1880–1980* (1988). She is the editor of *Signs about Signs: The Semiotics of Self-Reference* (1980) and *The Reversible World: Essays on Symbolic Inversion* (1978).

DAVID P. BILLINGTON is professor of civil engineering and operations research at Princeton University. He was educated at Princeton University and at universities in Louvain and in Ghent in Belgium, and has been a visiting professor at Cornell University. He worked as an architect specializing in bridge design and also pioneered in the teaching of structural art and interdisciplinary studies combining engineering, architecture, and the humanities. He is the author of *Robert Maillart and the Art of Reinforced Con-*

crete (1990) and *The Tower and the Bridge: The New Art of Structural Engineering* (1983).

CHRISTIAN BLANCHET, a former member of the French diplomatic service, worked for more than three years with his former collaborator Bertrand Dard in preparing both the French- and the English-language versions of a book on the Statue of Liberty. The French version, *Statue de la Liberté: Le Livre du centenaire,* was published in 1985 by Edition Comet in Paris, while the English version appeared in 1985 as *Statue of Liberty: The First Hundred Years* (Bernard A. Weisberger, translator), published in New York by American Heritage Publishing Company. Together, Blanchet and Dard examined more than ten thousand documents, interviewed more than a thousand persons, and visited more than a hundred museums, libraries, and private collections to pay homage to "La Grande Dame de New York." Their work produced a traveling exhibition on the statue, as well as a television film. In Paris, Blanchet now is an officer of Union Latine, an international, intergovernmental organization of twenty-five states with the purpose of promoting "Latinity" through various forms of cultural diplomacy.

BERTRAND DARD is the coauthor, with Christian Blanchet, of a richly illustrated centennial book on the Statue of Liberty, published in both French and English versions. His work as a graphic designer of exhibitions drew heavily on his previous experience as a collector and connoisseur of posters and antiques. Ambassador François de Laboulaye, a descendant of the nineteenth-century statesman who originated the idea of the gift of Liberty to the United States, praised the centennial book as "a reference of the first order." In 1985, the Académie Française awarded the book its history prize. Dard, along with Christian Blanchet, also organized a highly successful exhibition on Edith Piaf, the chanteuse, on the twentieth anniversary of her death.

WILTON S. DILLON, senior scholar in residence at the Smithsonian Institution, was educated at the University of California at Berkeley, Columbia University, Musée de l'Homme in Paris, and the University of Leyden in The Netherlands. He is the former director of the Smithsonian's Office of Interdisciplinary Studies. He wrote *Gifts and Nations* (1968), edited *The Cultural Drama* (1974), and coedited (with J. F. Eisenberg) *Man and Beast* (1971). He has been honored in France with the Chevalier des Arts et des Lettres for his contributions to French-American relations.

SEYMOUR DRESCHER is University Professor of History at the University of Pittsburgh. He was educated at the City College of New York and the University of Wisconsin (Ph.D. in history, 1960). He has taught at Harvard

University, Carnegie-Mellon University, and the Graduate Center of the City University of New York. He served as secretary of the European Program at the Woodrow Wilson International Center for Scholars. He is the author of *Capitalism and Antislavery: British Mobilization in Comparative Perspective* (1987) and *Tocqueville and England* (1964), editor of *Political Symbolism in Modern Europe* (1982) and *Tocqueville and Beaumont on Social Reform* (1968), and coeditor (with Frank McGlynn) of *The Meaning of Freedom: Economics, Politics, and Culture after Slavery* (1992).

FANG LI ZHI is professor of physics and astronomy at the University of Arizona in Tucson. He was educated at Peking (Beijing) University. His research work embraces nuclear reactor theory, solid state physics, and laser physics. He has held several teaching and university administrative posts in China and was elected a member of the Chinese Academy of Sciences. During the cultural revolution in the People's Republic of China, Dr. Fang was sent to the countryside to work on a communal farm and in a coal mine. He became a prominent advocate of intellectual freedom and human rights in China. At the time of the student-led pro-democracy demonstrations in Beijing in 1987, Dr. Fang and his wife narrowly escaped arrest and sought sanctuary in the U.S. embassy in Beijing, where they lived for one year. After arriving in the United States in 1990, he served as a research fellow at the Institute for Advanced Study in Princeton. He is the author of numerous articles and books on science and philosophy, including *Creation of the Universe* (1989), *Philosophy as a Tool of Physics* (1989), and *Bringing Down the Great Wall: Writings on Science, Culture, and Democracy in China* (1992).

NEIL G. KOTLER is a special assistant in the Smithsonian's Office of External Affairs. He was educated at Brandeis University, the University of Wisconsin, and The University of Chicago (Ph.D., political science, 1974). He served for ten years as a legislative assistant in the U.S. House of Representatives and taught American government, international relations, and political thought at DePaul University, Dartmouth College, the University of Texas, and Georgetown University. He served as a Peace Corps volunteer in Asmara, Ethiopia. He has edited several books for the Smithsonian Institution Press, including *Frontiers of Nutrition and Food Security in Asia, Africa, and Latin America* (1992), *Sharing Innovation: Global Perspectives on Food, Agriculture, and Rural Development* (1990), and *Completing the Food Chain: Strategies for Combating Hunger and Malnutrition* (1989).

JOHN J. MACALOON is associate professor of the social sciences and a member of the Committee on Social Thought at The University of Chicago. Educated at the Catholic University of America and The University of

Chicago (Ph.D., 1980), he is the author of *This Great Symbol: Pierre de Cou-bertin and the Origins of the Modern Olympic Games* (1981) and the editor of *General Education in the Social Sciences: Centennial Reflections on the College at The University of Chicago* (1992) and *Rite, Drama, Festival, Spectacle: Re-hearsals toward a Theory of Cultural Performance* (1984). He has written two other books that are scheduled for publication: *Sport Discourse and American Politics: Explorations in the Sociology of Culture* and *Brides of Victory: National-ism and Gender in Olympic Ritual.*

TSAO HSINGYUAN is a sculptor, art historian, and Asia scholar living in California. She was educated at the Zhejiang Academy of Fine Arts in Hangzhou and the Central Academy of Fine Arts in Beijing, People's Re-public of China (M.A., 1988). After arriving in the United States in the late 1980s, Tsao was trained in Asian studies at the University of California at Berkeley (M.A., 1991) and is currently enrolled in a Ph.D. program at Stan-ford University. She has taught art in middle and secondary schools and has lectured on aesthetics and art history at Jilin University, Bethune Medical College, Northeast Normal College, and Changchun Geography Universi-ty. She holds a research appointment in the Institute of Art Research, Acad-emy of Arts of China, in Beijing. Tsao's sculptures and paintings have been the subject of exhibitions, and several are on view in Changchun and Hangzhou.

RUDOLPH J. VECOLI is professor of history and director of the Immi-gration History Research Center at the University of Minnesota. He was educated at the University of Connecticut, the University of Pennsylvania, and the University of Wisconsin (Ph.D., 1963). His teaching appointments have included Ohio State University, Pennsylvania State University, Rut-gers University, and the University of Illinois. He has served as president of the Immigration History Society and the American Italian Historical Asso-ciation. He is a coeditor (with Suzanne Sinke) of *A Century of European Mi-gration* (1991), author of the article "The Invention of Ethnicity: A Per-spective from the U.S.A." (1990), editor of and a contributor to *Italian Immigrants in Rural and Small Town America* (1987), and author of *The Peo-ple of New Jersey* (1965).